LEADING DYNAMIC INFORMATION LITERACY PROGRAMS

T0384876

Leading Dynamic Information Literacy Programs delves into the library instruction coordinator's work. Each chapter is written by practicing coordinators, who share their experiences leading information literacy programs that are nimble, responsive, and supportive of student learning.

The volume discusses the work of instruction coordinators within five thematic areas: Claiming Our Space: Library Instruction in the Landscape of Higher Education; Moving and Growing Together; Curriculum Development; Meaningful Assessment; and Leading Change. Readers will gain insight from their colleagues' advice for situating information literacy within the higher education institution, developing meaningful curricula, and using assessment in productive ways. Many of the stories represent a departure from traditional models of library instruction. In addition, this book is sure to spark inspiration for innovative approaches to program leadership and development, including strategies for growing communities of practice.

From leadership skills and techniques, methods for cultivating shared values, pedagogical approaches, team building, assessment strategies – and everything in between – the aspiring or practicing instruction coordinator has much to gain from reading this work.

Anne C. Behler is Information Literacy Librarian and Instruction Coordinator for the Library Learning Services department of the Penn State University Libraries, where she leads curriculum innovation for foundational information literacy instruction. Behler's recent scholarship explores instruction delivery strategies and leading instruction communities of practice.

LEADING DYNAMIC INFORMATION LITERACY PROGRAMS

Best Practices and Stories from Instruction Coordinators

Edited by Anne C. Behler

Routledge
Taylor & Francis Group

LONDON AND NEW YORK

Cover image: © Getty images

First published 2023
by Routledge
4 Park Square, Milton Park, Abingdon, Oxon OX14 4RN

and by Routledge
605 Third Avenue, New York, NY 10158

Routledge is an imprint of the Taylor & Francis Group, an informa business

© 2023 selection and editorial matter, Anne C. Behler; individual chapters, the contributors

British Library Cataloguing-in-Publication Data
A catalogue record for this book is available from the British Library

ISBN: 978-0-367-48197-1 (hbk)
ISBN: 978-0-367-46279-6 (pbk)
ISBN: 978-1-003-03863-4 (ebk)

DOI: 10.4324/9781003038634

Typeset in Bembo
by MPS Limited, Dehradun

This book is dedicated to the woman-leaders in my life, who have taken the time to share their knowledge, and who use their positions to clear a path for the success of other women.

– Anne C. Behler

CONTENTS

List of Figures   *ix*
List of Tables   *x*
List of Contributors   *xi*

Introduction
Anne C. Behler   1

PART I
Claiming Our Space: Library Instruction in the
Landscape of Higher Education   **7**

1   Navigating a Shifting Landscape: Information Literacy in
    Higher Education
    Clarence Maybee   9

2   Situating Information Literacy within the Institution:
    Building a Dynamic Program
    Mary C. MacDonald   26

PART II
Moving and Growing Together   **43**

3   Program Foundations: Establishing Values, Boundaries, and
    Priorities
    Rebecca Miller Waltz   45

4   From Individual to Community: Building a Community of
     Practice around Teaching   64
     Rachel W. Gammons, Yelena Luckert, Anastasia Armendariz,
     and Lindsay Inge Carpenter

PART III
Curriculum Development   **83**

5   Instruction by Design: Embedding the Library into
     Curriculum Design   85
     Rachel I. Wightman

6   The Right Tools for the Job: Integrating a Variety of
     Instructional Modes into an Information Literacy Program   98
     Dani Brecher Cook

PART IV
Meaningful Assessment   **115**

7   Improving Information Literacy Instruction through
     Programmatic Student Learning Assessment   117
     Maoria J. Kirker and Ashley Blinstrub

PART V
Leading Change   **135**

8   That's Not the Way We've Always Done It: Coordinating
     Research Instruction with Innovation, Teamwork,
     Assessment, and Collaboration   137
     Emily Z. Brown and Susan Souza-Mort

9   Time for a Reboot! Making Space for Instruction Program
     Development   150
     Anne C. Behler

Appendix 1: Example Applications of Unique Library Instruction
           Integrations at Bristol Community College   162
Appendix 2: Email Announcing Reboot to ENGL 15 Instructors   165
Index   167

FIGURES

3.1   Sample RACI chart   54
6.1   Introductory STEM courses pathway   102
6.2   The learning pathway through the three courses, developed in
       consultation with the relevant academic department coordinators   103
6.3   An example of "the Atoms" setting the stage for the module
       learning outcomes, by struggling to find a copy of their course
       textbook   105
6.4   Outline for the *CRC Handbook* module   106
6.5   A screenshot from the CHEM 01LA tutorial demonstrating
       common reference sources   106
6.6   A screenshot demonstrating the importance of reliable reference
       sources   107
6.7   A screenshot from the BIOL 05LA module introducing the
       concept of "thinking like a scientist"   108
6.8   NASC modules required students to successfully complete a
       short quiz   110
9.1   A recipe for successful partnerships   159

TABLES

1.1 'Frames' of the ACRL *Framework for Information Literacy in Higher Education*   18

7.1 Example learning outcomes, corresponding to ascending levels of topic mastery   130

8.1 Bristol Community College Assessment Rubric   141

CONTRIBUTORS

Anastasia Armendariz is the librarian for special collections and the Malibu historical collection at Pepperdine Libraries. She serves as the associate editor for the Teaching with Primary Sources (TPS) Collective's open peer-reviewed blog, *Notes from the Field*.

Ashley Blinstrub is the student success and inclusion librarian at George Mason University. She has her MS in information from the University of Michigan.

Anne C. Behler is the information literacy librarian and instruction coordinator for the Library Learning Services department of the Penn State University Libraries, where she leads curriculum innovation and development for foundational information literacy instruction. Behler is an active member of the Association for College & Research Libraries (ACRL) and Council for Adult and Experiential Learning (CAEL).

Emily Z. Brown is the coordinator of library research and instruction at Bristol Community College.

Lindsay Inge Carpenter is the pedagogy librarian and research education program lead at the University of Maryland Libraries. She is also the subject specialist for the Second Language Acquisition Department and provides leadership of UMD Libraries' OER program, as well as co-directing the UMD Libraries' Research and Teaching Fellowship.

Dani Brecher Cook is the associate university librarian for learning and user experience at the UC San Diego Library. She previously held positions related to instruction at the UC Riverside Library and the Claremont Colleges Library.

Rachel W. Gammons is the head of teaching and learning services at the University of Maryland Libraries, where she provides leadership for the Libraries' information literacy instruction program, supervises a team of teaching librarians and staff, and serves as codirector of the UMD Libraries' Research and Teaching Fellowship. She is a Ph.D. candidate in higher education, student affairs, and international education policy at the University of Maryland.

Maoria J. Kirker is the teaching and learning team lead at George Mason University Libraries. Before becoming team lead, she served as the instruction and assessment coordinator for Mason Libraries. She holds an MSLIS from the University of Illinois at Urbana-Champaign and an MS in educational psychology from George Mason University.

Yelena Luckert is the director of research, teaching, and learning at the University of Maryland Libraries, where she provides leadership in policy creation, development, implementation, strategic planning, and assessment for the Libraries' liaison librarians program, and the research, reference, and teaching operations. In addition, Ms. Luckert is the subject specialist librarian for Jewish and Slavic Studies.

Mary C. MacDonald is the head of instructional services at the Carothers Library, University of Rhode Island, where she oversees several information literacy instruction programs, including a set of credit bearing general education information literacy courses. Mary has served on several ACRL Instruction Section committees and taught for the ACRL Immersion Program. She received the 2017 ACRL Instruction Section Miriam Dudley Instruction Award.

Clarence Maybee is a professor and the W. Wayne Booker Chair in Information Literacy at Purdue University. He regularly publishes and presents on information literacy and is author of the book *IMPACT Learning: Librarians at the Forefront of Change in Higher Education*.

Susan Souza-Mort is a research and instruction librarian and coordinator of library services in New Bedford for Bristol Community College.

Rebecca Miller Waltz is the associate dean for learning and undergraduate services at Penn State University Libraries. Through her professional roles, Rebecca has led the collaborative creation of a new vision, strategic plan, and scope of work for the teaching and learning departments at two different libraries. A 2012 ALA Emerging Leader and a 2016 Harvard Leadership Institute for Academic Librarians alum, Rebecca is deeply engaged with the profession and has served in leadership roles with the American Library Association (ALA), ACRL, and LOEX. She has also served as an ACRL Information Literacy Immersion Program facilitator and written and presented widely on the topics of teaching and learning, learning spaces, and library leadership.

Rachel I. Wightman is the associate director for instruction and outreach at Concordia University, St. Paul.

INTRODUCTION

Anne C. Behler

In 1974, when library instruction as a concept was in its infancy, Allan J. Dyson undertook a study of the variety of ways library instruction was being formalized within the library as an organization. His findings then were that library instruction was typically arranged in one of four ways. The first was "underground" library instruction, a model that has hopefully disappeared by now. In this model, there was no administrative support for instruction though the public services librarians felt it important and likely went ahead and offered classes, on top of their other duties. In another administrative model, there might be a designated instruction librarian – one – who spent 100% of their time on teaching with little or no staff support. Dyson mentions two other models, which more closely resemble today's library instruction programs. The first engages all of an institution's librarians in instruction without naming anyone as an instruction librarian, while the second utilizes instruction librarian(s) as coordinators of instruction for the institution (1974).

What I find remarkable about Dyson's work, which is now over 45 years old, is that the structures he uncovered clearly planted the seeds for the ways our current library instruction programs tend to be organized. Indeed the "sample job description" he offered as a template for hiring instruction coordinators could be adapted and used today. It reads:

> The Library Instruction Coordinator ... is responsible for the initiation, development, and evaluation of a coordinated program of library instruction. He/she is responsible for keeping abreast of the latest developments in library instruction including audio-visual innovations and for making recommendations to improve the library's orientation and instructional programs. (appendix 1)

DOI: 10.4324/9781003038634-1

Replace "audio-visual" with the more modern terms *learning and classroom technology,* and that description could be published in a job ad today. The instruction coordinator position is clearly an institution unto itself.

However, while the job title, description, and the structure around it may remain similar today, the landscape in which instruction coordinators work has most certainly changed. The LOEX organization has been vigilant in tracking many of these cultural shifts through surveys of the field, conducted every decade or so. It's clear that the emergence of the Web and non-print information tools in the 1990s served as a catalyst for both change in the library classroom and the formation of a stronger community among instruction librarians. The Web enabled quick information sharing through listservs, such as BI-L, a phenomenon that was new as of the 1995 study of library instruction trends (Shirato & Badics, 1997). Even as the documented need for library instruction and training was on the rise in the 1990s, the administrative structure around it, in most cases, remained lacklustre. Shirato and Badics (1997) noted:

> The vast majority of instruction programs are still administered by the reference department or public services, just as they have been in the past. Many hardly seem to be administered at all – some responded that the library director administered the program, or that it was a shared responsibility. Only a few libraries ... have a separate department for library instruction, even when there is a full-time coordinator. (p. 226)

Also noteworthy from this 1995 survey is that, despite the seeming disorganization of library teaching, 76% of the institutions who responded to the survey indicated that there was one person in charge of instruction. It was not, however, typically that person's only job. Only 11% of those "in charge of instruction" focused full-time on instruction and administration of instruction (Shirato & Badics, 1997). Clearly, things have changed since 1997. Many libraries include an instruction department or employ a dedicated instruction coordinator, though this role, new as it is, still has much room for interpretation.

Perhaps, then, it is unsurprising that even today there is a dearth of guidance for those who find themselves in the instruction coordinator role. The organizers of the 2001 LOEX Library Instruction Conference, titled *Managing Library Instruction Programs in Academic Libraries,* noted this of their own conference stating, "It's been twenty-six years since LOEX last had an explicit focus on management" (Petrowski, 2001, pg. 3). In her introduction to the conference proceedings, Petrowski (2001) notes that helpful resources had been developed since 1975, when library instruction programs were beginning. Among them she highlights several efforts by the Association for College & Research Libraries (ACRL) to guide the development of these programs. Documents such as the ACRL *Information Literacy Competency Standards for Higher Education* and the *Framework for Information literacy in Higher Education* and programs like the ACRL Immersion Program have been instrumental in guiding instruction coordinators toward building instructional programs that make an impact for the students who pass through. But the job of instruction coordinator reaches farther than the teaching, beyond the curriculum development. As Petrowski (2001) remarks, "IL program managers (and those who aspire to be managers) are directly and indirectly responsible for moving the library and the campus forward in some of the most important areas" (pp. 3–4).

What an exciting and important position to find oneself in! Indeed, the library instruction coordinator holds the responsibility for guiding how information literacy and fluency take shape at their institution. Doing so includes developing and managing partnerships, guiding or responding to curriculum developments, managing or leading other teaching librarians, keeping abreast of current pedagogies, and quite often working to mindfully integrate social awareness and/or justice into the library classroom.

Unfortunately, as noted by Mary C. MacDonald in her 2008 book chapter about program management, "outside of a possible management course in library school, many information literacy program managers are unprepared for the myriad of tasks that await them as coordinators or managers of an IL program" (Cox & Lindsay, 2008, pg. 113). ACRL's *Standards for Proficiencies for Instruction Librarians and Coordinators: A Practical Guide* (2008) offers a detailed list of skills that the "effective coordinator" must be able to carry out. These are skills that hearken back to, and expand upon, Dyson's original job description template.

And so, we instruction coordinators are not without some guidance as to *what* we ought to be able to accomplish. The question, it seems, is *how*. As with many roles within our profession, it is a combination of experiences and guidance from colleagues that give possibility and life to the various components that come together to form the role of instruction coordinator. It is the editor's hope that this book and the personal experiences of leadership therein equip the reader with a better sense of how the job can be approached, and the impact that a job well done can have on the information literacy program for the entire institution.

The contributors to this book share experience and guidance that give possibility and life to the various components that form the role of instruction coordinator. We begin by "claiming our space" within higher education, and within the institution. Clarence Maybee shows us how the higher education conversation about information literacy has evolved, both shaping our library instruction programs and the institutions in which we work. He encourages us to look to past models and practices, even as we strive to "oversee [programs that are] ever evolving and responsive to the new ideas about information literacy." Mary C. MacDonald then takes a deep dive into how the models and practices within higher education can serve as "anchors" as we work to situate information literacy within our individual institutions.

Next, we consider ways that we can develop and lead a teaching program that is flexible, collaborative, and responsive to student needs. Rebecca Miller Waltz gives guidance on building a team that is mission and vision-focused, in a psychologically safe space. A team of librarians from the University of Maryland share their story of program growth and development through forming a community of practice that includes implementation of two teacher training programs. Rachel I. Wightman and Dani Brecher Cook follow with chapters that encourage us to be flexible and adaptable when considering how best to design our curriculum. Wightman offers a model that situates the library directly at the center of all curriculum design for the university, while Cook encourages us to consider what modes of instruction enable us to be nimble and responsive to curricular needs, while ensuring student learning. In both cases, collaboration and innovation win the day.

Assessment can underpin all of our efforts as instruction coordinators. Indeed, each chapter of this book offers an example of how formal or informal assessment can aid us in situating our instructional programs, making curricular decisions, and allocating our program resources. In chapter seven, Kirker and Blinstrub guide us through the process of creating, implementing, and revising a student learning assessment plan. This plan has aided the librarians at George Mason University in flexing their library instruction program to assess and meet student learning needs.

Another theme that runs through each chapter of this book is that of instruction coordinator as change leader. The final two chapters – one from a community college, one from a large research university – tell stories of instruction program evolution. Each institution has taken a unique and deliberate approach to changing the direction of their library instruction. Brown and Souza-Mort share their story of re-energizing a stagnant library instruction program by engaging their instruction librarians and the broader campus community in information literacy that is embedded in the curriculum and campus culture, rather than being limited to one-shot instruction. Finally, the editor shares her own story of leading change by taking the radical step to stop library instruction for a semester in order to make space and time for a program "reboot."

Space and time are a concept that deserve a special mention here. While the common threads among these chapters are many, one that surprised me – though it shouldn't have – is that each and every story told herein represents many years of work. Program development is, indeed, an evolutionary process. Whether one is examining a piece of the program, or the entire program itself, change is incremental and cumulative. The instruction coordinator must have their eye on both levels, and as the micro- and macro-levels of growth come together, a story can be told. I am grateful to the authors who contributed to this book and took their valuable time to share their stories.

References

Association of College and Research Libraries. (2008). *Standards for proficiencies for instruction librarians and coordinators: A practical guide.* American Library Association. http://acrl.ala.org/IS/wp-content/uploads/2014/05/profstandards.pdf

Dyson, A.J. (1974). *Organizing undergraduate library instruction: The English and American experience (ED152309).* ERIC.

MacDonald, M.C. (2008). Program management. In C.N. Cox & E.B. Lindsay (Eds.), *Information literacy instruction handbook*. Association of College and Research Libraries.

Petrowski, M.J. (2001). Managing information. In J.K. Nims & E. Owen (Eds.), *Managing library instruction programs in academic libraries: Selected papers presented at the twenty-ninth national LOEX library instruction conference*. Perian Press.

Shirato, L., & Badics, J. (1997). Library instruction in the 1990s: A comparison with trends in two earlier LOEX surveys. *Research Strategies, 4*(15), 223–237. 10.1016/S0734-331 0(97)90011-2

PART I
Claiming Our Space: Library Instruction in the Landscape of Higher Education

1

NAVIGATING A SHIFTING LANDSCAPE: INFORMATION LITERACY IN HIGHER EDUCATION

Clarence Maybee

Introduction

Since 2004, I have been an instruction coordinator in academic libraries at three different higher education institutions—two liberal arts colleges and one large research university. During this time, I have witnessed a plethora of ideas about information literacy come and go! These ideas have included new ways of conceptualizing information literacy derived from scholarship, such as new research findings or exploring theoretical perspectives (Accardi et al., 2010; Bruce, 2008; Lloyd, 2010), but also big events in the field, such as the introduction of the *Framework for Information Literacy in Higher Education* (the *Framework*) (Association of College & Research Libraries [ACRL], 2015). Additional discussions occurred about various other kinds of information-focused literacies, such as media literacy (Center for Media Literacy, n.d.) or transliteracy (Thomas et al., 2007), which some in the library community thought should guide our instructional programs. This chapter outlines the changing ideas of information literacy over the past several decades and explores how these developments have informed the work of instruction coordinators, including myself, in shaping information literacy programs.

Origins

It was an amazing privilege to hear Paul Zurkowski, the founder of the concept of 'information literacy,' deliver the keynote address at the European Information Literacy Conference in 2013. Zurkowski told the audience that while he may have coined the term 'information literacy' (Zurkowski, 1974), he was impressed with what the library community had done with it over the proceeding decades. In defining information literacy, Zurkowski gave shape to a nascent idea emerging in the academic library community that they needed to shift their efforts to help

DOI: 10.4324/9781003038634-3

the students, faculty, and staff at their institutions find and make sense of the print and online information resources they provided and organized.

In 1987, the American Library Association (ALA) appointed a Presidential Committee on Information Literacy, which produced a report espousing the role of information literacy in engendering enterprise and democracy (American Library Association [ALA], 1989). The report describes an information literate person as someone able to "recognize when information is needed and have the ability to locate, evaluate, and use effectively the needed information" (p. 1). Also called for in the report, the National Forum on Information Literacy (NFIL) was created. The Forum was led by library luminary, Patricia Senn Breivik, and her colleagues, including Lana Jackman and Sharon Weiner.

As a testament to the growing global significance of information literacy, in 2003, the National Forum on Information Literacy (NFIL), together with the United Nations Educational, Scientific and Cultural Organization (UNESCO) and National Commission on Libraries and Information Science (NCLIS), sponsored an international conference in Prague to discuss the importance of information literacy within a global context. The work of this group resulted in the Prague Declaration (2003), which identified information literacy as "key to social, cultural, and economic development of nations, communities, institutions, and individuals in the 21st century."

From the standpoint of the instruction coordinator, national and even international recognition of the role it could play in economics and civic life provided a justification for information literacy programs aimed at enabling learners that would be successful after graduation. When the concept of information literacy was first introduced, it sparked debate amongst librarians, whose teaching practice until that time was called, 'bibliographic instruction,' and focused solely on training library users to locate materials. Becoming more common in the second half of the twentieth century, bibliographic instruction was provided in one form or another dating back to before the American Civil War (Salony, 1995). Instruction coordinators developing library instruction programs had to make the case for information literacy, pointing out the difference between it and bibliographic instruction, as well as explaining its significance to stakeholders across their institutions. In many ways, the early work to introduce information literacy to the world and academia shaped how it has been understood, researched, and practiced since. From this starting point, there is not one story of information literacy to tell, but several, as information literacy was explored through research and the development of educational practice.

The Standardization Years

Now that several years have passed, I wonder if academic librarians new to the profession can imagine the role that the *Information Literacy Competency Standards for Higher Education* (the *Standards*) played in the development of information literacy in higher education. From 2000 to 2015, *The Standards* provided a definition of information literacy that guided most of the information literacy programs in the

United States. The *Standards* described an information literate student as possessing select information skills that would enable them to

- determine the nature and extent of the information needed,
- access needed information effectively and efficiently,
- evaluate information and its sources critically and incorporate selected information into his or her knowledge base and value system,
- individually or as a member of a group, use information effectively to accomplish a specific purpose, and
- understand many of the economic, legal, and social issues surrounding the use of information and accesses and uses information ethically and legally (ACRL, 2000).

A testament to their reach, over the years, the *Standards* were used as the starting point to develop new standards to guide the information literacy instruction provided by liaisons working with courses in various disciplines, including anthropology, sociology, journalism, teacher education, and nursing (ACRL, 2008, 2011a, 2011b, 2013). Beyond librarianship, the *Standards* (ACRL, 2000) also informed the description of information literacy in the Value Assessment of Learning in Undergraduate Education (VALUE) Rubric for Information Literacy created by the Association of American Colleges and Universities (AACU, n.d.) and guidelines put out by regional accrediting agencies (Middle States Commission on Higher Education [MSCHE], 2009; New England Association of Schools and Colleges [NEASC], 2005; Western Association of Schools and Colleges [WASC], 2008). The *Standards* (ACRL, 2000) also influenced the development of information literacy standards in other countries, including Australia (Bundy, 2004) and Great Britain (Society of College, National and University Libraries [SCONUL], 2011).

When I became the information literacy librarian at Mills College in 2004, there was a clear expectation from the library's administrators that the *Standards* (ACRL, 2000) would guide the programming that I developed. At that time, the small staff of librarians offered little instruction, although the library did provide a 1-credit information literacy course each spring. There was, however, recognition from some stakeholders on campus of the importance of information literacy. Looking for co-curricular options, library administrators suggested having students complete an information literacy tutorial as an efficient way to reach all students.

A few years later, it became common for libraries to create their own online tutorials to serve a variety of needs, such as database training, introduction to library services, and issues related to information ethics (Yang, 2009), outline a process or even explain contextual aspects of using information (Sundin, 2008). However, at Mills College in 2004, we had few resources to create a tutorial on our own. Like many other academic libraries, we selected the Texas Information Literacy Tutorial (TILT), which was freely available on the Internet and allowed for adaptation. The TILT tutorial emphasized skills closely aligned with those outlined in the ACRL *Standards* (2000). I spent a summer working with a couple other library staff to adapt the TILT tutorial for the Mills context. The new tutorial, called Mills Information Literacy Evaluation (M.I.L.E.), became a requirement for all Mills students.

As a new librarian with the responsibility for developing the Mills information literacy instructional offerings, I was not satisfied with only having students engage with the M.I.L.E. tutorial. I wanted to bring information literacy to students in the classroom. I explored the literature describing how information literacy coordinators frequently partnered with composition programs (McMillen et al., 2002; Samson & Millet, 2003), and thought this a possible pathway. I met with the coordinator of the composition program and pitched the idea to embed lessons into first-year composition courses. She bounced the idea off the group of English faculty members who advised the program, and they agreed that the information literacy lessons would be beneficial for students. I worked with another librarian to design the lessons and a corresponding rubric. I originally intended for the instructors, many of them adjuncts, to teach the lessons, but the faculty advisors to the composition program insisted that the librarians lead the sessions. Designed with the *Standards* (ACRL, 2000) in mind, the lessons took place across a semester and were designed to enable students to locate and evaluate information for a final paper.

As an instruction coordinator developing programming during the time of the *Standards* (ACRL, 2000), I often felt that they constrained information literacy teaching practice. Some researchers have made a similar assertion, suggesting that the pervasive application of the *Standards* to define information literacy in research projects limited what those studies were able to explore (Lundh et al., 2013). At the same time, I recognized that the *Standards* provided a certain authority to our work (Drabinski & Sitar, 2016), and for many librarians rescinding them was extremely problematic. Over time I have come to the realization that it was not the existence of the *Standards* (ACRL, 2000) that hampered instructional practice, but how they were applied within librarianship. In most fields, standards represent a sub-set of knowledge and skills that guide what students at certain levels are expected to learn about the discipline. In librarianship, at least in practice, the *Standards* became the de facto definition of the entirety of information literacy, setting up a barrier to the exploration and teaching about aspects of information literacy that went beyond that which was described in the *Standards*.

The Assessment Mandate

Beginning her book on information literacy assessment, Teresa Neely (2006) stated, "It follows that once standards for student learning have been established, the focus logically turns to assessment" (p. 2). Both activities, that is, creating the standards and developing information literacy assessment plans, may be viewed as part of the greater assessment movement in higher education, what Emily Drabinski (2017) has referred to as the "time of compliance." This movement had a most significant impact on the work of information literacy instruction coordinators who strove to determine and implement ways of assessing students' capabilities with and perceptions of information literacy at a programmatic level. When I first became a librarian in 2005, there were several librarians writing about how to develop assessment plans and learn more about assessment strategies. Resources targeted both individual librarians, many of whom were new to teaching and needed to learn about classroom assessment techniques, as well as instruction coordinators, who needed to learn about assessing at the programmatic level (Lindauer, 2004; Oakleaf, 2008; Radcliff et al., 2007).

A 2009 review of 91 articles revealed that the two most frequently used assessment methods were multiple choice tests (34%, n = 31), and analysis of bibliographies (19%, n = 17) (Walsh, 2009). We used bibliographic analysis in the project at Mills College in which information literacy lessons were embedded into composition courses. A team of three librarians applied a rubric, based primarily on the *Standards* (ACRL, 2000), to evaluate the bibliographies from students' final papers to determine if they used appropriate sources to address the information need described in their paper's thesis. By doing this assessment, separate from the classroom instructors' evaluation, the library was able to get a snapshot of students' capabilities related to information literacy, which we used to adjust the program as well as report out to campus stakeholders, such as the faculty overseeing the composition program.

With some exceptions, such as providing sustained teaching in general education programs, libraries typically do not have access to the majority of students through classroom interactions. Therefore, a common approach to information literacy assessment has been standardized testing, which can be administered outside of curricular efforts. Perhaps the most well-known of these tests is Project SAILS, but there are many others, such as Information Literacy Self-Efficacy Scale (ILSES), and the Information Literacy Test (ILT) (Mahmood, 2017), to name a few. Most of the existing tests focus on concepts like those outlined in the ACRL *Standards* (2000), although tests are being developed that do not draw from the *Standards*, such as the Threshold Achievement Test for Information Literacy (TATIL), which is based on the ACRL *Framework* (2015).

Largely because they reflected the *Standards* (ACRL, 2000), which I thought were too limiting, I have not encouraged the institutions I have worked for to implement any of the existing standardized tests. That said, when I was at Colgate University, I worked with my campus to have students participate in one of the early Project Information Literacy (PIL) studies, which surveyed undergraduates at 25 institutions about their use of information to complete research assignments (Head & Eisenberg, 2010). Although research and not assessment, the local findings were indeed useful for highlighting the importance of information literacy to stakeholders. My skepticism of the usefulness of standardized information literacy tests led me to consider developing one for use at Purdue University, my current institution, that better aligned with our local approach to information literacy. Aligned with our theoretical perspective, colleagues at Purdue and I developed a scale that gauges students' perceptions of how they use information in their courses to learn (Flierl et al., 2021).

Other Literacies

While the ACRL definition of information literacy outlined by the *Standards* (ACRL, 2000) dominated our work in higher education, numerous other information-related literacy models and theories have been introduced over time. Some have even promised to replace information literacy! For example, after arriving at my office at Colgate University one spring day in 2010, one of my colleagues popped in to ask me if I had heard of 'transliteracy' (Thomas et al., 2007). I was told that transliteracy was a new approach to 'literacy' that was going to replace information literacy. In the coming months, I heard the same from other colleagues as well. I was, to put it mildly, intrigued. What was this concept that was going to replace information literacy and thus upend my efforts at Colgate?

I began reading about transliteracy, and I attended a local conference, titled the "3 T's: Exploring New Frontiers in Teaching, Technology and Transliteracy Conference" held at Fulton Montgomery Community College in 2011. Founded by Sue Thomas, transliteracy focuses on reading, writing, and interacting across platforms through a variety of media, including handwriting, print, TV, radio, and film (Thomas, 2008; Thomas et al., 2009). Transliteracy suggests that innovation is best supported not by the movement of information with a single network, but rather the interplay of information between social networks. To informally gauge the application of transliteracy in librarianship, Koltay (2011) interviewed librarians working in different sectors about their knowledge of the theory, and although they thought the theory had merit, only the academic librarian was familiar with transliteracy prior to the interview. While still being used by librarians (Sukovic, 2016), ten years later transliteracy has yet to replace the concept of information literacy in higher education.

Other concepts that have been closely related to information literacy are 'media literacy' and 'digital literacy,' and efforts have been made to examine the borders between information literacy and other types of literacies (Bawden, 2001; Koltay, 2011). Media literacy focuses on locating and evaluating media content and understanding the role of media in society (Center for Media Literacy, n.d.). The United Nations Educational, Scientific and Cultural Organization (UNESCO) formed a new model called, 'Media and Information Literacy' (MIL) that integrates ideas from both information literacy and media literacy (United Nations Educational, Scientific and Cultural Organization [UNESCO], 2016).

Digital literacy raises similar concerns to both information and media literacies, but also focuses on digital tools and communicating and collaborating in digital environments. JISC of the United Kingdom (JISC, n.d.) has created a framework defining digital literacy that includes

- basic skills,
- using information, data, and media,
- creating digital products,

- participating in online groups,
- teaching and learning in digital environments, and
- digital identity and well-being.

Grounded in the JISC model, the University Libraries at Virginia Tech (2019) developed the *Digital Literacy Framework Toolkit* to promote digital literacy on their campus. In the JISC construction, information literacy is one of many ideas that are part of digital literacy (JISC, n.d.). In sharp contrast, Jacobson and Mackey (2011) suggest that information literacy is an overarching framework that encompasses other information-focused literacies, including media literacy and digital literacy. Their model is now part of the ACRL *Framework* (2015).

Despite the differences, groups vying for the advancement of one or another literacy often compete for the same institutional resources. At Purdue, the focus for many years has been on information literacy, which became a foundational learning outcome in our campus-wide core curriculum approved by the Faculty Senate in 2012. As such, there are several courses across campus that meet the information literacy core outcome. The Libraries have been directly involved with many of these courses, working with departmental instructors to ensure that the courses meet the core criteria. One of the courses is offered by the Libraries. Another, which is offered by another department, is exclusively taught by librarians. That said, there have been recent conversations at the state level about the importance of digital literacy as an outcome for graduates of Indiana institutions.

It is a part of the job of an instruction coordinator to stay abreast of the information literacy-related discussions on their campuses and in the field. A major lesson for me was to place less emphasis on prognostications, like whether information literacy will be replaced by another literacy, and instead focus on what might be learned from new theories and ideas. Rather than viewing them as challenges, evolving campus interests in different literacies can be in dialog with information literacy, supporting the development of responsive programming.

Other Approaches to Information Literacy

While many theories and frameworks are used to guide information literacy research projects (Lloyd, 2021) as well as the creation of individual instructional experiences, this is less common in the framing of programmatic efforts. Programmatic offerings and assessment are typically framed by the ACRL *Framework* (2015) or other frameworks offered by library or education advocacy organizations (AACU, n.d.; Bundy, 2004; SCONUL, 2011). Much of the programming I have coordinated at Colgate and Purdue has focused on working with disciplinary faculty to integrate information literacy into the curriculum. While the *Framework* (ACRL, 2015) may be used to do this kind of work (Wishkoski et al., 2018), I believe that two other models, 'community of practice'

(Lloyd, 2010) and 'informed learning' (Bruce, 2008), especially lend themselves to addressing information literacy within disciplinary contexts.

The community of practice approach views learning as a process of en-culturation that occurs through participation in activities that enable a student to recognize the tacit practices taking place within the learning environment (Lave & Wenger, 1991). From a community of practice perspective, information literacy is a 'situated' practice that typically occurs in 'real life' settings, such as the workplace (Lloyd, 2010). So, while a community of practice approach to information literacy may produce transformative learning experiences, in higher education, it is most suited to learning environments that enact or simulate authentic learning, such as internships, practicums or service learning.

In contrast to a community of practice approach, informed learning (Bruce, 2008) also emphasizes using information within disciplinary contexts but is less dependent on authentic situations. I began to explore informed learning when I was at Colgate and later made it an important component of our information literacy efforts at Purdue. Developed by Australian researcher Christine Bruce[1], informed learning is an approach to information literacy that emphasizes 'learning' as the outcome of using information. The central idea of informed learning is that learning to use information and learning about subject content (e.g., disciplinary facts, theories, skills, etc.) should occur at the same time. It is guided by three principles:

- Builds on learners' current experience with using information in learning contexts
- Promotes simultaneous learning about subject content and information use
- Enables learners to experience both information use and subject content in new ways (Bruce & Hughes, 2010)

Based on earlier research, three frameworks were developed over time that are integral to informed learning (Bruce, 2008). Derived from Bruce's dissertation research, the 'seven faces' framework describes different experiences educators may have of information literacy (Bruce, 1997). The GeST windows model (Lupton & Bruce, 2010) outlines different approaches to information literacy:

- generic (skills and processes)
- situated (authentic disciplinary and professional), and
- transformative (critical perspective).

The Six Frames (Bruce et al., 2006) is a pedagogic model that draws from major approaches taken in teaching and delineates how information literacy is typically represented in those approaches. From their own perspectives, each of the three frameworks suggest that teaching and learning that focuses on creating new knowledge or personal or social development is frequently associated with more complex ways of using information.

Informed learning (Bruce, 2008) has been used to design coursework as well as to inform strategies for liaisons working within various departments (Ranger, 2019). At Purdue, informed learning has been used to describe how our instructional programs focus on disciplinary learning as an outcome of using information. It guides the Purdue Libraries' efforts in a campus-wide faculty development program that I coordinate with leaders from our teaching center and technology unit (Maybee, 2018). The program, which was started in 2011, focuses on creating engaging and motivating learning environments. Most undergraduate students at Purdue have taken at least one course that was redesigned through the program (Levesque-Bristol et al., 2019). Librarians work with instructors to help them create learning activities in which students use information to learn disciplinary content. Informed learning also guides several related programs hosted by the Libraries, such as a one-day workshop to develop information literacy assignments, and a program in which instructors create projects that help students learn about using data in disciplinary contexts, such as retail management or political science (Maybee et al., 2021).

To guide our collaboration with classroom instructors to integrate information literacy, I developed 'informed learning design,' a design model that specifically focuses on enabling students to learn to use information in disciplinary learning environments (Maybee et al., 2019). My group at Purdue received funding from the Institute of Museum and Library Services to conduct a project in which 15 teams of librarians and instructors from the University of Arizona, University of Nebraska, Lincoln, and Purdue University (5 teams at each university) are applying informed learning design to create student projects for undergraduates to learn to use information in disciplinary learning contexts (Maybee, 2019–2023). Drawing on their own experiences working with students, the librarians involved in the project were able to use the steps of the design process to guide the instructors in the development of responsive learning activities that enabled the students to use information to be successful in the course.

The Framework

During the development of the *Framework for Information Literacy for Higher Education* (ACRL, 2015), I held open sessions with librarians at Purdue to discuss the latest drafts. When filed in 2015 and adopted in early 2016 by the ACRL Board, I was hopeful that the broader definition of information literacy espoused in the *Framework* would encourage more expansive ways of teaching higher education students about using information. Grounded in the two concepts of 'metaliteracy' and 'threshold concepts,' the *Framework* both defines information literacy broadly and provides specific targets for student learning.

The metaliteracy model draws together technology-related literacies, such as media and digital literacies, under the umbrella of information literacy (Jacobson & Mackey, 2011). Threshold concepts theory suggests that certain concepts pose barriers that are 'thresholds' to be attained before further learning can occur

(Meyer & Land, 2003). The finding from research exploring threshold concepts for information literacy (Hofer et al., 2013) informed the new *Framework's* (ACRL, 2015) six information-related concepts to guide information literacy educational offerings in higher education (see Table 1.1).

TABLE 1.1 'Frames' of the ACRL *Framework for Information Literacy in Higher Education*

Frame	Description
Scholarship is a Conversation	Emphasizes sustained discourse within a community of scholars or thinkers, with new insights and discoveries occurring over time as a result of competing perspectives and interpretations.
Research as Inquiry	Describes research as iterative and that it depends upon asking increasingly complex questions whose answers may develop new questions or lines of inquiry.
Format as Process	Focuses on processes of developing information sources that originate from different needs, motivations, values, conventions, and practices, and appear in different formats, and suggests that the underlying questions about value of the information and its potential use are more significant than the physical packaging of the information source.
Authority is Constructed and Contextual	Highlights the variation in information quality that may be needed for a given purpose and the types of evaluative criteria to apply in specific contexts. It also encourages an attitude of informed skepticism towards trusting the authority of that information, as well as remaining open to new perspectives, additional voices, and changes in schools of thought.
Searching as Exploration	Focuses on searching and locating information and involves defining an information need, knowing possible tools, collections, and repositories that may be useful in locating information, using and refining appropriate search vocabularies and protocols to design specific search strategies.
Information has Value	Acknowledges that the creation of information and products derived from information require a commitment of time, original thought, and resources that need to be respected by those seeking to use those products or create their own based on the work of others. Information may be highly valued based on its creator, its audience/consumer, or its message.

Source: Adapted from ACRL, 2015.

Emily Drabinski and Meghan Sitar (2016) argue that the *Framework* (ACRL, 2015) is also a set of standards, even if that is not the view held by the librarians who composed it. Certainly, the *Framework* is used to guide the development of coursework (Bravender et al., 2015) and assessment (Gammons et al., 2017; Oakleaf, 2014). The Libraries at Purdue did not use the *Standards* (ACRL, 2000) at a programmatic level to assess information literacy instruction, and we did not adopt the *Framework* (ACRL, 2015) for that purpose either. Our model, which values instructor autonomy, supports librarians choosing their own information literacy theories or models to guide their instructional efforts. Nevertheless, several Purdue librarians do use the *Framework* when designing their instruction. While still providing specific targets for instruction, I believe that the *Framework* is broad enough to allow libraries and individual librarians to teach content that is relevant to the needs and interests of the students and faculty working within various disciplines.

Critical Information Literacy

Critical approaches have been evolving in scholarly conversations as well as librarians' instructional practice over the decades since the introduction of information literacy in higher education. Grounded in ideas drawn primarily from critical pedagogy (Freire, 1993; hooks, 2014), many critiques have been offered of information literacy research and practice, especially as framed by the *Standards* (ACRL, 2000). For example, Christine Pawley (2003) examined the historical uses of the words 'information' and 'literacy' and questioned the viability of the democratic empowerment that advocates claimed would result from information literacy. Cushla Kapitzke (2003) offered a poststructuralist critique suggesting that the linear and hierarchical approaches typically employed did not address the social and political aspects to information literacy. Drawing from Freire (1993), James Elmborg (2006) called for librarians to reassess their own identity from a critical perspective, to recognize the library as value-laden and socially constructed, which would inform a critical approach in their teaching practice.

Conferences, journals, and listservs have been developed to provide the academic library community spaces to discuss critical approaches to information literacy. Eamon Tewell (2015, 2018) has done work to identify specific practices librarians use, as well as the articles and books that have been important in presenting theories, models, and instructional work grounded in a critical perspective. Introduced in 2010, *Critical Library Instruction: Theories and Methods* (Accardi et al., 2010) was a very influential book that opened a door for many librarians to consider critical approaches by outlining theories used in critical pedagogy and instructional methods applied in critical information literacy instruction. Another instrumental book for librarians wishing to explore critical approaches to information literacy is the two-volume set, *Critical Library Pedagogy Handbook, Essays and Workbook Activities,* edited by Nicole Pagowsky and Kelly McElroy (2016), which shares teaching practices and lesson plans.

At Purdue, like many academic libraries, we are just beginning to consider how to address critical perspectives programmatically. Purdue librarians are attending conferences and other trainings on inclusion and equity in instruction. I led a workshop series last year on creating equitable online learning environments. Individual librarians have been heavily involved in the creation of the Critical Data Studies Collective, a campus-wide community of scholars dedicated to advancing curricula and research that focuses critical perspectives to explore and use data. Purdue librarians are also developing new courses that examine information and data literacy from critical perspectives, including an introductory undergraduate course. The large-scale faculty development program that the Libraries hosts with key partners has shifted to work with classroom instructors to enable them to create inclusive learning environments for students, which includes considering the oppressive structures in place. There is growing recognition across the Libraries that a critical perspective should guide our instructional efforts.

In contrast to the ACRL *Standards* (2000), there is recognition that the *Framework* (ACRL, 2015) lends itself to a more critical perspective for understanding and assessing our information environment (Drabinski, 2017; Saunders, 2017). While there is more work to be done, such as addressing systemic racism (Rapchak, 2019), the ability of the *Framework* (ACRL, 2015) to both foster critical approaches to instruction and 'frame' information literacy within higher education makes it a useful tool for instruction coordinators advancing critical information literacy programming.

Concluding Thoughts

It seems clear that the work of an instruction coordinator rests on the amazing contributions of our peers who have gone before—those who first brought the idea of information literacy to life, those who made it an integral part of their institutions, and those who worked through so many possible ways of thinking about information literacy—all for the purpose of enabling our students to be able to navigate and learn within today's complex and occasionally hazardous information environment. For me, the *Framework* (ACRL, 2015) has provided more latitude in how we can arrange our instructional programs to address local needs. Critical approaches that inform both our teaching and learning strategies and what we teach students about how information is created and used in our societies are essential.

We should also continue to apply ideas derived from information literacy research and scholarly practice. For example, I plan to explore how a critical lens can be applied within the informed learning framework (Bruce, 2008) to guide our faculty development work at Purdue. Over the years I have wondered, as have others (Owusu-Ansah, 2005), if the conversation about the nature of information literacy would die down at some point. Now I think that was not the right question to ask. Instead, I believe the work of the instruction coordinator and the programs we oversee need to be ever evolving and responsive to the new ideas about information literacy. This is not to say that we need to bring them all into our work but that instruction programs, when possible, should include a space for experimentation. One thing seems certain: future research and scholarly practice will produce new ideas about information literacy, and we owe it to our students, and to ourselves, to explore those ideas and, if appropriate, apply them to advance student learning at our institutions.

Note

1 Professor Bruce was my doctoral advisor in the Gateway program offered through a partnership between San José State University and Queensland University of Technology in which I studied experiences of informed learning in an undergraduate writing course.

References

Accardi, M.T., Drabinski, E., & Kumbier, A. (Eds.). (2010). *Critical library instruction: Theories and methods.* Library Juice Press.

American Library Association. (1989). *Final Report.* https://www.ala.org/acrl/publications/whitepapers/presidential

Association of American Colleges and Universities. (n.d.). *Information literacy VALUE rubric.* http://www.aacu.org/value/rubrics/information-literacy

Association of College and Research Libraries. (2000). *Information literacy competency standards for higher education.* Association of College and Research Libraries.

Association of College and Research Libraries. (2008). *Information literacy competency standards for anthropology and sociology students.* http://www.ala.org/acrl/standards/anthro_soc_standards

Association of College and Research Libraries. (2011a). *Information literacy competency standards for journalism students and professionals.* http://www.ala.org/acrl/sites/ala.org.acrl/files/content/standards/il_journalism.pdf

Association of College and Research Libraries. (2011b). *Information literacy competency standards for teacher education.* EBSS Instruction for Educators Committee. http://www.ala.org/acrl/sites/ala.org.acrl/files/content/standards/ilstandards_te.pdf

Association of College and Research Libraries. (2013). *Information literacy competency standards for nursing.* http://www.ala.org/acrl/standards/nursing

Association of College and Research Libraries. (2015). *Framework for information literacy for higher education.* http://www.ala.org/acrl/standards/ilframework

Bawden, D. (2001). Information and digital literacies: A review of concepts. *Progress in Documentation, 57*(2), 218–259. 10.1108/EUM0000000007083

Bravender, P., McClure, H., & Schaub, G. (2015). *Teaching information literacy threshold concepts: Lesson plans for librarians.* Association of College and Research Libraries.

Bruce, C.S. (1997). *The seven faces of information literacy.* Auslib Press.

Bruce, C.S. (2008). *Informed learning.* American Library Association.

Bruce, C.S., Edwards, S.L., & Lupton, M. (2006). Six frames for information literacy education: A conceptual framework for interpreting the relationships between theory and practice. *Innovations in Teaching and Learning Information and Computer Sciences, 51*(1), 1–18. 10.11120/ital.2006.05010002

Bruce, C.S., & Hughes, H. (2010). Informed learning: A pedagogical construct attending simultaneously to information use and learning. *Library and Information Science Research*, *32*(4), A2–A8. 10.1016/j.lisr.2010.07.013

Bundy, A. (2004). *Australian and New Zealand information literacy framework: Principles, standards and practice*. Australian and New Zealand Institute for Information Literacy.

Center for Media Literacy. (n.d.). *Mdia literacy: A definition and more*. Retrieved October 17, 2021, from http://www.medialit.org/media-literacy-definition-and-more/

Drabinski, E. (2017). A kairos of the critical: Teaching critically in a time of compliance. *Communications in Information Literacy*, *11*(1), 76–94. 10.15760/comminfolit.2017.11.1.35

Drabinski, E., & Sitar, M. (2016). What standards do and what they don't. In N. Pagowsky & K. McElroy (Eds.), *Critical library pedagogy handbook* (Vol. 1, pp. 53–64). Association of College and Research Libraries.

Elmborg, J. (2006). Critical information literacy: Implications for instructional practice. *Journal of Academic Librarianship*, *32*(2), 192–199. 10.1016/j.acalib.2005.12.004

Flierl, M., Bonem, E., & Maybee, C. (2021). Developing the informed learning scale: Measuring information literacy in higher education. *College & Research Libraries*, *82*(7), 1004–1016. 10.5860/crl.82.7.1004

Freire, P. (1993). *Pedagogy of the oppressed* (New rev 20th-Anniversary). Continuum.

Gammons, R.W., & Inge, L.T. (2017). Using the ACRL Framework to develop a student-centered model for program-level assessment. *Communications in Information Literacy*, *11*(1), 168–184. 10.15760/comminfolit.2017.11.1.40

Head, A.J., & Eisenberg, M. (2010). *Project Information Literacy progress report: Truth be told: How college students evaluate and use information in the digital age*. University of Washington's Information School. http://projectinfolit.org/publications/

Hofer, A.R., Brunetti, K., & Townsend, L. (2013). A threshold concepts approach to the standards revisions. *Communications in Information Literacy*, *7*(2), 108–113. 10.15760/comminfolit.2013.7.2.141

hooks, bell. (2014). *Teaching to transgress*. Routledge. 10.4324/9780203700280

JISC. (n.d.). *What is digital capability?* Retrieved October 17, 2021, from https://digitalcapability.jisc.ac.uk/what-is-digital-capability/

Kapitzke, C. (2003). Information literacy: A review and poststructural critique. *Australian Journal of Language and Literacy*, *26*(1), 53–66.

Koltay, T. (2011). The media and the literacies: Media literacy, information literacy, digital literacy. *Media, Culture & Society*, *33*(2), 211–221. 10.1177/0163443710393382

Lave, J., & Wenger, E. (1991). *Situated learning: Legitimate peripheral participation*. Cambridge University Press.

Levesque-Bristol, C., Maybee, C., Parker, L.C., Zywicki, C., Connor, C., & Flierl, M. (2019). Shifting culture: Professional development through academic course transformation. *Change*, *51*(1), 35–41. 10.1080/00091383.2019.1547077

Lindauer, B.G. (2004). The three arenas of information literacy assessment. *Reference & User Services Quarterly*, *44*(2), 122–129. https://www.jstor.org/stable/20864327

Lloyd, A. (2010). *Information literacy landscapes: Information literacy in education, workplace and everyday contexts*. Chandos.

Lloyd, A. (2021). *The qualitative landscape of information literacy research: Perspectives, methods and techniques*. Facet.

Lundh, A.H., Limberg, L., & Lloyd, A. (2013). Swapping settings: Researching information literacy in workplace and in educational contexts. *Information Research*, *18*(3). http://InformationR.net/ir/18-3/colis/paperC05.html

Lupton, M., & Bruce, C.S. (2010). Windows on information literacy worlds: Generic, situated and transformative perspectives. In A. Lloyd & S. Talja (Eds.), *Practising information literacy: Bringing theories of learning, practice and information literacy together* (pp. 4–27). Charles Sturt University. 10.1016/B978-1-876938-79-6.50001-7

Mackey, T.P., & Jacobson, T.E. (2011). Reframing information literacy as a metaliteracy. *College and Research Libraries, 72*(1), 62–78. 10.5860/crl-76r1

Mahmood, K. (2017). Reliability and validity of self-efficacy scales assessing students' information literacy skills. *The Electronic Library, 35*(5), 1035–1051. 10.1108/EL-03-2016-0056

Maybee, C. (Principal Investigator). (2019–2023). *Academic librarian curriculum developers: Building capacity to integrate information literacy across the university* (Project No. RE-13–19-0021-19). [Grant]. Institute for Museum and Library Services. https://www.imls.gov/sites/default/files//grants/re-13–19-0021-19/proposals/re-13–19-0021-19-full-proposal.pdf

Maybee, C. (2018). *IMPACT learning: Librarians at the forefront of change in higher education.* Chandos.

Maybee, C., Bruce, C.S., Lupton, M., & Pang, M.F. (2019). Informed learning design: Teaching and learning through engagement with information. *Higher Education Research & Development, 38*(3), 579–593. 10.1080/07294360.2018.1545748

Maybee, C., Lin, G., Cai, C., Fitzsimmons, J., & Sun, Y. (2021). Building undergraduate data literacy through faculty development. In J. Bauder (Ed.), *Teaching critical thinking with numbers: Data literacy and the Framework for Information Literacy for Higher Education.* ALA Editions.

McMillen, P.S., Miyagishima, B., & Maughan, L.S. (2002). Lessons learned about developing and coordinating an instruction program with freshman composition. *Reference Services Review, 30*(4), 288–299. 10.1108/00907320210451277

Meyer, J.H.F., & Land, R. (2003). Threshold concepts and troublesome knowledge: Linkages to ways of thinking and practising within the disciplines. In C. Rust (Ed.), *Improving student learning theory and practice—10 years on* (pp. 412–424). Oxford Brookes University.

Middle States Commission on Higher Education. (2009). *Characteristics of excellence in higher education requirements of affiliation and standards for accreditation.* Middle States Commission on Higher Education. https://web.jhu.edu/administration/provost/reaccreditation/_template_assets/docs/MSCHE%20Characteristics%20of%20Excellence.pdf

New England Association of Schools and Colleges. (2005). *Standards for accreditation.* New England Association of Schools and Colleges Commission on Institutions of Higher Education.

Neely, T.Y. (2006). *Information literacy assessment: Standards-based tools and assignments.* American Library Association.

Oakleaf, M. (2008). Dangers and opportunities: A conceptual map of information literacy assessment approaches. *Portal: Libraries and the Academy, 8*(3), 233–253. 10.1353/pla.0.0011

Oakleaf, M. (2014). A roadmap for assessing student learning using the new Framework for Information Literacy for Higher Education. *The Journal of Academic Librarianship, 40*(5), 510–514. 10.1016/j.acalib.2014.08.001

Owusu-Ansah, E.K. (2005). Debating definitions of information literacy: Enough is enough! *Library Review, 54*(6), 366–374. 10.1108/00242530510605494

Pagowsky, N., & McElroy, K. (2016). *Critical library pedagogy handbook, essays, and workbook activities (Vols. 1 & 2).* Association of College and Research Libraries.

24 Clarence Maybee

Pawley, C. (2003). Information literacy: A contradictory coupling. *The Library Quarterly*, *73*(4), 422–452.

Prague Declaration. (2003). *Prague declaration: Towards an information literate society*. https://ar.unesco.org/sites/default/files/praguedeclaration.pdf

Radcliff, C.J., Jensen, M.L., Salem, Jr., J.A., Burhanna, K.J., & Gedeon, J.A. (2007). *A practical guide to information literacy assessment for academic librarians*. Libraries Unlimited.

Ranger, K.L. (2019). *Informed learning applications: Insights from research and practice*. Emerald Publishing.

Rapchak, M. (2019). That which cannot be named: The absence of race in the Framework for Information Literacy for Higher Education. *Journal of Radical Librarianship*, *5*, 173–196. https://journal.radicallibrarianship.org/index.php/journal/article/view/33

Salony, M.F. (1995). The history of bibliographic instruction: Changing trends from books to the electronic world. *The Reference Librarian*, *24*(51–52), 31–51. 10.1300/J120v24n51_06

Samson, S., & Millet, M.S. (2003). The learning environment: First-year students, teaching assistants, and information literacy. *Research Strategies*, *19*(2), 84–98. 10.1016/j.resstr.2004.02.001

Saunders, L. (2017). Connecting information literacy and social justice: Why and how. *Communications in Information Literacy*, *11*(1), 55–75. 10.15760/comminfolit.2017.11.1.47

Society of College, National and University Libraries. (2011). *SCONUL seven pillars of information literacy: Core model for higher education*. https://www.sconul.ac.uk/page/seven-pillars-of-information-literacy

Sukovic, S. (2016). *Transliteracy in complex information environments*. Chandos.

Sundin, O. (2008). Negotiations on information-seeking expertise: A study of web-based tutorials for information literacy. *Journal of Documentation*, *64*(1), 24–44. 10.1108/00220410810844141

Tewell, E. (2015). A decade of critical information literacy: A review of the literature. *Communications in Information Literacy*, *9*(1), 24–43. 10.15760/comminfolit.2015.9.1.174

Tewell, E. (2018). The practice and promise of critical information literacy: Academic librarians' involvement in critical library instruction. *College & Research Libraries*, *79*(1), 10–34. 10.5860/crl.79.1.10

Thomas, S. (2008). Transliteracy and new media. In Adams, R., Gibson, S., & Arisona, S.M. (Eds.), *Transdisciplinary digital art: Sound, vision and the new screen* (pp. 101–109). Springer.

Thomas, S., Joseph, C., Laccetti, J., Mason, B., Mills, S., Perril, S., & Pullinger, K. (2007). Transliteracy: Crossing divides. *First Monday*, *12*(12). 10.5210/fm.v12i12.2060

Thomas, S., Joseph, C., Laccetti, J., Mason, B., Perril, S., & Pullinger, K. (2009). Transliteracy as a unifying perspective. In Hatzipanagos, S., & Warburton, S. (Eds.), *Handbook of research on social software and developing community ontologies* (pp. 448–465). IGI Global.

United Nations Educational, Scientific and Cultural Organization. (2016, September 1). *Media and Information Literacy*. https://en.unesco.org/themes/media-and-information-literacy

University Libraries, Virginia Tech. (2019). *Digital Literacy Framework toolkit*. https://odyssey.lib.vt.edu/s/home/item/256

Walsh, A. (2009). Information literacy assessment: Where do we start? *Journal of Librarianship & Information Science*, *41*(1), 19–28. 10.1177/0961000608099896

Western Association of Schools and Colleges. (2008). *Handbook of accreditation 2008*. Western Association of Schools and Colleges. https://wasc.cetys.mx/initial/docs/support/Handbook_of_Accreditation_2008_with_hyperlinks.pdf

Wishkoski, R., Lundstrom, K., & Davis, E. (2018). Librarians in the lead: A case for interdisciplinary faculty collaboration on assignment design. *Communications in Information Literacy, 12*(2), 166–192. 10.15760/comminfolit.2018.12.2.7

Yang, S. (2009). Information literacy online tutorials: An introduction to rationale and technological tools in tutorial creation. *The Electronic Library, 27*(4), 684–693. 10.1108/02640470910979624

Zurkowski, P.G. (1974). *The information service environment relationships and priorities. Related Paper No. 5.* (ED100391). ERIC. https://eric.ed.gov/?id=ED100391

2

SITUATING INFORMATION LITERACY WITHIN THE INSTITUTION: BUILDING A DYNAMIC PROGRAM

Mary C. MacDonald

Introduction

How do libraries develop information literacy (IL) programs that stand the test of time, through administration, staffing, and curriculum changes? What situates IL within an institution of higher education so that the institution identifies, recognizes, and values the program? Academic instruction librarians, whether part of the team, or identified as coordinators, unit heads, or managers, are tasked with achieving the goal of providing opportunities whereby their communities can become information literate. Optimally, the goal is to reach as many students, faculty, and staff as possible through as many varieties of instruction and outreach as possible within the framework of the academic library and the academic institution. How then, do we approach such an enormous goal? IL is a vast content area and matching the needs of your institution to the varied facets of IL requires a skilled team of librarians using their strengths as strategists, pedagogists, and information technologists.

This chapter will discuss how the instruction librarians and their coordinator at the University of Rhode Island (URI) used conventional elements and expectations of higher education to build and maintain their IL program for over twenty years. Three university presidents, four library deans, and shifting staff changes over this period shaped both the rewards and challenges of beginning, growing, and sustaining our program. Instruction coordinators will recognize these elements and expectations as mainstay structures, or anchors, found in academic programs across higher education.

The chapter will also include examples of IL program experiences from other college and university libraries. Brief interviews conducted with librarians from these institutions will show what factors keep their programs vital to the institution, the libraries, and the students. Instruction coordinators know the challenges

DOI: 10.4324/9781003038634-4

of how to create and sustain their IL programs; it is my hope that the URI story and these examples will fortify your efforts as you continue to create programs that empower student research, and sometimes, remind you of why we persevere.

Finding Our Anchors

Shapiro and Hughes' "Information Literacy as a Liberal Art" (1996), provided an early inspiration that encouraged us to seek broad sources of evidence that support our desire to create an assessable, scaffolded program in place of a scattershot attempt at fulfilling student needs. The authors asserted,

> Information literacy should in fact be conceived more broadly as a new liberal art that extends from knowing how to use computers and access information to critical reflection on the nature of information itself, its technical infrastructure, and its social, cultural and even philosophical context and impact – as essential to the mental framework of the educated information age citizen as the trivium of basic liberal arts (grammar, logic and rhetoric) was to the educated person in medieval society.

Shapiro and Hughes identified the information literacy landscape as a subject worthy of learning at the college level. To be an educated citizen, one should be experienced with the process of information creation, be able to identify the political and social aspects that influence information, and finally be able to find, evaluate, use, and share information. Seeking the anchors to support the IL plan we had in mind for the URI community, we first looked to the university's mission statement, and later, the General Education Program goals. We intended that the URI community would see how being IL competent is essential to becoming an experienced and savvy researcher.

The University of Rhode Island Mission Statement (1996) asserted that "The university is committed to providing strong undergraduate programs to promote students' ethical development and capabilities as critical and independent thinkers." The University Libraries Mission Statement (1994) directly reinforced the URI mission, by stating specifically how we would support student success, including via instruction and collaboration with faculty:

> The University Libraries support the success of students, faculty and researchers through *instruction*, access, preservation, and innovation ... Library faculty provide materials and services across campuses, *including providing for-credit instruction, collaborating with faculty across disciplines to provide targeted class-specific instruction*, and selecting print and electronic resources in accordance with the university's mission.

The University Libraries vision statement (1994) further underscored this notion, by emphasizing the librarians' role as partners in teaching, research, and service, stating, "As partners in the teaching, research, and service missions of the university, the libraries will continue to acquire, organize, and preserve materials in all formats and provide instruction in their use."

Beyond the University of Rhode Island, we looked to guiding documents from the American Library Association (ALA), American Association of School Librarians (AASL), and the Association of College and Research Libraries (ACRL). These early documents were strong supports for the program model we envisioned. For example, the 1989 *American Library Association Presidential Committee on Information Literacy: Final Report* on IL states:

> What is called for is not a new information studies curriculum but, rather, a restructuring of the learning process … Such a restructuring of the learning process will not only enhance the critical thinking skills of students but will also empower them for lifelong learning and the effective performance of professional and civic responsibilities.

Before ACRL promulgated the first *Information Literacy Standards for Higher Education*, in 2000, we used a position paper from the AASL to strengthen our stance with URI administrators:

> To be prepared for a future characterized by change, students must learn to think rationally and creatively, solve problems, manage and retrieve information, and communicate effectively. By mastering information problem-solving, students will be ready for an information-based society and a technological workplace.

Information literacy is a necessary, and often overlooked, learning content area. Our efforts to establish IL as more than just 'library instruction' moved slowly, but we did gain ground every few years. Library instruction coordinators will recognize many of the hurdles we faced but will also identify our rewards, though many were long in coming. The work of developing a place for IL in the higher education curriculum is long term but invaluable for students. An IL curriculum benefits the entire institution as its graduates go forth to careers and professions knowing how to find and, most importantly, evaluate information. The ongoing concern about citizens' ability to discern bias, propaganda, misinformation and disinformation is another support to turn to in the advocacy for IL programs at any institution of learning.

Information Literacy Course Development

I was working a reference desk shift at the URI University Library (now the Carothers Library) in fall 1997, when I was approached by a student in desperate need of assistance. The student explained that they had been downstairs in the new computer lab working on a research paper about Timothy McVeigh's 1994 bombing of the Oklahoma federal building and could not find reliable information sources on the web. The student's plea was clear: "No one down there can help me, can you?" Sensing frustration in the student's voice I left the desk and followed them to the computer lab to explain how to use the new databases. After helping that student, I turned and saw a dozen or more hands raised, asking for similar help. While I felt elated after helping so many, I was left with the question: Who is helping them learn to do online research? Clearly there was a need for more student support.

Long before I became part of the URI Library faculty, the URI University Libraries' Public Services Department had provided library instruction. Since the mid-1960s, URI librarians had offered fall library orientations, 'one shot' instruction for subject specific courses, and summer instruction sessions for the Talent Development Program (https://web.uri.edu/talentdevelopment/). In the mid-1990s I was simultaneously both a student in the URI Graduate School of Library and Information Studies (GSLIS) and a URI Library paraprofessional employee. URI faculty librarians regaled GSLIS students with accounts of instruction happenings prior to our arrival on the scene. Instruction requests grew fast and furious in the later 1990s due to the explosive increase in use of internet sources by students and faculty. Faculty were amazed at the amount of information now available at their fingertips. Students were equally thrilled with the vast amounts of available information but lacked the skill set to use the Internet for college level research. URI's library instruction program needed to become more robust; this became even more obvious when the librarians realized just how much more support students needed to apply critical thinking and analysis to internet sources. We had the capacity to offer plenty of reference and instruction services and we did, but in reflection we realized that our approach was a bit scattershot. First- and second-year students were the primary beneficiaries of our teaching efforts. Moreover, some academic majors had professors who more readily requested library instruction, causing their students to experience duplicative efforts. When I was hired as a librarian in 1997, the Public Services department consisted of five tenured faculty librarians and three lecturer librarians. The department also hired a half-dozen graduate students from the URI GSLIS each academic year. The graduate students were trained to staff the reference desk as well as teach introductory classes. Soon we were brainstorming about how to update our library instruction methods and content, as well as how to increase and scale the delivery of instruction services so that we could reach as many of the approximately fourteen-thousand students enrolled at URI (University of Rhode Island, n.d.b). In short, we needed to determine what more we could offer to support students in this new age of information research.

Not long after my eye-opening reference desk shift, the Library Dean asked us to consider developing a three-credit IL course. The dean was relatively new to URI but quickly recognized the need for increased library instruction due to the onset of internet research, and he called for more robust initiatives. For the 1998/1999 academic year, library instruction statistics included 325 instruction sessions for 7,325 students, reaching approximately half the enrolled student body. Still, the dean was in favor of developing a credit-bearing course that would teach students the concepts and skills of IL in order to support them in their work. We knew that we had to deliver much more content to many more students. What formats, logistics, and permissions would be necessary to achieve our goal? We all agreed that students needed more experience and practice with information research strategies to become more sophisticated researchers. Teaching a credit-bearing course would provide this opportunity, and the course itself would become an example when making the argument that IL is a worthy and valuable subject for the overall university curriculum. It would be exciting for us as librarians, but we knew it would stretch us to capacity. Almost everyone was on board, and those that were not, were at least willing to let us try.

With great excitement, two librarians sitting on a bus during the 1998 American Library Association drafted the first syllabus proposal on the back of an envelope. After consulting with campus curriculum experts, we proposed two elective courses: LIB 120: Introduction to Information Literacy, a three-credit course, and LIB 140: Special Topics in Information Literacy, a one-credit course. LIB 140 was meant to be taught alongside a subject content course, and the content of LIB 140 would be tailored to meet the information needs of that discipline or program.

LIB 120 would cover the basic concepts of information formats, search, evaluation, and use. Employing active learning and authentic assignments, students could begin to understand the landscape of information, learn strategies for searching both print and online sources, and develop their own research questions to practice and apply these strategies. Students would create an information research project and provide authentic evidence of their research path. I call this process "finding the mud" of research. Too often students submit beautiful, finished products to their professors, but the professor hasn't asked for the evidence of the research done. Both courses would have the goal of developing students' ability to identify, practice, and apply critical thinking and analysis of finding and evaluating sources. With fine-tuning and fierce department and university review, both course proposals were accepted, and our credit-bearing course teaching careers began.

In discussing this process, it is important to note that URI librarians hold faculty status. This allows us to be elected or appointed as voting members of the Faculty Senate and University-wide committees, and this has given us leverage in steering the course of the IL program. Over the years, Public Service Department faculty librarians have been members of the University Curriculum Committee, General Education Committee, faculty senators, and even Faculty Senate President. Being able to independently submit course proposals to our faculty senate and to teach credit-bearing courses in university curricula without having other units or departments as sponsors has given us both advantages and responsibilities. However, faculty status is not the linchpin for an IL program; the IL program must identify, prove, and fulfill an identified need. At URI, even with course approval, we still had to accomplish this task.

The LIB 120 course was taught first at our extension campus, with low student enrollment. We wrestled with how we could encourage students to give the course a chance. We then collaborated with an encouraging and supportive business professor, who desired stronger research skills in his students. We co-enrolled students from two sections of his MGT 110: Introduction to Business course in two sections of LIB 140: Special Topics in Information Literacy. Through this experience, we were able to test our content and teaching on two classes of novice researchers—first-year students from the College of Business. This endeavor was satisfactory in terms of teaching subject-specific IL to college first-year students; however, enrolling students in the course became logistically difficult due to the numerous other requirements for this program of study. Shortly thereafter, this same faculty member suggested that we propose our elective three-credit course as part of the University's General Education Program. All URI undergraduate students are required to complete a general education program, and the faculty member recognized that more students should benefit from an LIB course. Following this advice, the course was proposed as such and soon became part of the General Education Program under the area of English Communication. This was a watershed moment for the URI LIB courses, and the IL program.

For over twenty years, our participation in General Education has been steady, even as that program itself has evolved. Our courses, (originally LIB 120 and LIB 140; now LIB 150, 250, and 350), have always found a home within this program, even as it has followed higher education shifts and trends. In the early planning days, our courses were approved for general education credit because they fit within English Communication and included "instructional technology." While this was just a small part of our overall course content, we were pleased that it helped us to stay within the approved scope of a general education course.

A revised general education program in 2005 was more aligned with IL, and thus linked us more closely with the university curriculum:

> Students, faculty, staff, and alumni are united in one common purpose: to learn and lead together. Embracing Rhode Island's heritage of independent thought, we value: Creativity and Scholarship, Diversity, Fairness, and Respect, Engaged Learning and Civic Involvement, and Intellectual and Ethical Leadership. (Endorsement of Mission Statement for the University of Rhode Island, 2005)

As the first learning outcomes were established for the General Education Program, the LIB 120 Introduction to Information Literacy course began to fit into the curriculum more naturally. The learning outcomes helped faculty recognize the value of the course, and students understood why they were taking the course. Librarians were pleased to see that all general education courses would expect that students be able to:

- identify basic concepts, theories, and developments;
- recognize issues, as well as aesthetic and literary elements and forms;
- ask questions appropriate to the modes of inquiry;
- collect information relevant to the questions raised; and
- analyze the information in order to address the questions or solve problems (University of Rhode Island, 2007–2008).

Once LIB 120 became an every-semester general education offering, we were able to offer more sections, reaching a high of thirteen sections at one point. Being a general education course meant guaranteed full enrollment in every section. Support from library administration allowed us to hire part-time evening librarians, freeing faculty librarians up for the heavier teaching load. LIB 120 was taught every semester, including summer. Generally, several sections were taught during the same semester. Colleagues collaborated by sharing pedagogy, technology, and classroom management experiences. We experimented with using a textbook for a few semesters until we decided against it because the information landscape was, and continues to be, such a moving target. By the time a text is published, the information in this field is already outdated. To keep instructional materials up to date, we created our own content for use in this course. We shared ideas and materials with each other for syllabi, lesson plans, activities, assignments, and assessments. We developed our teaching styles so that classes and assignments utilized active learning tied to both formative and summative assessments. This helped us improve lesson plans—sometimes on the fly—and to identify what worked well, and where we needed to improve. We were learning how to teach in real time.

What a long way we had come from the first experience of teaching to the business students. In 1998, I learned quickly that I needed an actual lesson plan to get through a class. I had been jotting down ideas on the back of an envelope before class, later adding times (in minutes) to each section. Having never taken an education class, I barely realized I was developing a rudimentary lesson plan. To help us grow as teaching practitioners, we took advantage of faculty development programs and local, regional, and national learning opportunities from ACRL National and ACRL-New England (https://www.ala.org/acrl/; https://acrlnec.org/). Two of us participated in the Program and Assessment Tracks, then offered by ACRL Immersion (https://www.ala.org/acrl/conferences/immersion).

As our teaching practices evolved, our other IL instruction programs also benefited. First year one-shot instruction shifted from 'show and tell' tours and 'button pushing' sessions to Cephalonian Method tours and hands-on student-centered discovery sessions. Library classes began to focus more on developing search strategies and evaluating results rather than simply finding the information.

All of these experiences advanced our teaching, gave us greater visibility and credibility on campus and, most importantly, helped our students to succeed!

From Course Development to Information Literacy Plan

Even as the general education LIB courses became a fixture at URI, we recognized that this was still but one piece of a larger IL picture. Early on, while developing the two courses, we also began thinking about our instruction as an IL program rather than disparate instruction efforts. We needed to coordinate *all* of our instructional activities in a holistic way. We also needed to make room for our short- and long-term development goals. In short, we needed a formal IL program at URI. As it turned out, this was no small task and it often seemed interminable. At times, it was difficult to discern any progress being made. However, while I do not have a citation for this, I clearly remember listening to Tom Kirk of Earlham College, at the 1998 ACRL national conference, say that any good library instruction program will take ten years to develop. I remember thinking what a relief it was to hear him say that—we had only recently been tasked with developing one IL course—and I knew there was much more work to be done beyond that course!

The IL plan's origins stem from a library strategic planning event in 2000. A small group including five librarians—a branch manager, a technical services librarian and three public services librarians from the URI main campus—became the Task Force for Teaching and Research. The group members self-selected during the strategic planning event and continued to develop the first IL program document, "Plan for Information Literacy at the University of Rhode Island" (Burkhardt et al., 2000). At the time, we felt somewhat adrift, and wanted to demonstrate to other faculty and the upper-level university administration how library instruction efforts supported all students, no matter in which discipline or program students were enrolled.

The task force worked to identify elements in higher education that supported our assertion that IL deserves a permanent place in the wider university curriculum. We again looked to foundational elements of higher education that support and drive traditional curriculum to serve as anchors to secure a place for IL in the campus wide curriculum. We had used some of these elements to prove the value of LIB 120, but now we saw that these could support an entire program. These anchors include the basics of teaching and pedagogy, student-centered learning, and the use of assessment as evidence of accomplishing both. IL skills align with critical thinking skills and thus to the essential learning of higher education institutions (which have direct appeal to other faculty and upper-level administration). On our campus, this meant alignment with the university's strategic plan and the goals and objectives of General Education. As outside higher education entities became more familiar to us, we also aligned with the American Association of Colleges & Universities (AAC&U) IL rubric (n.d.), the ACRL *Information Literacy Standards for Higher Education* (*The Standards*) (2000), and then the *Framework for Information Literacy for Higher Education* (*The Framework*) (2015).

Other valuable anchors at URI include the accreditation criteria of our regional higher education accrediting body, the New England Association of Schools & Colleges (NEASC) (now the New England Commission of Higher Education (NECHE); the mission and vision statements of the university and those of the University Libraries. Together, these anchors have worked to situate, grow, maintain, and sustain the information literacy program for the period from 1998 to the present.

The first Plan for Information Literacy included the following program components, (although not all of our ambitions were realized at that time): subject specific bibliographic instruction, credit courses, integrated modules, web-based instruction materials such as tutorials, and consultations with faculty for assignment design (Burkhardt et al., 2000). Soon after we began teaching our new credit courses, the ACRL formalized and promulgated the *Information Literacy Competency Standards for Higher Education* (ACRL, 2000). This document became the gold standard for many IL instruction programs including ours, and we used it as a guide for IL instruction, but also as a declaration that we were in alignment with national library trends. It was rewarding to see that anchors we identified early in our program's development were soon included in the 2003 ACRL document, *Characteristics of Programs of Information Literacy that Illustrate Best Practices: A Guideline [Best Practices]* (ACRL, 2019). The ACRL document was richer and more fully articulated than our original URI IL plan, but it matched many of our considerations. The *Best Practices* categories include Mission, Goals and Objectives, Planning, Administrative, Program Sequencing, Pedagogy, Communication and Advocacy, and Assessment and Evaluation. These characteristics, or categories, reinforced the ideas we had been working with to develop and grow our program and helped us to further define areas of strength and weakness over the course of time.

Writing the IL plan helped to clarify our goals both for ourselves as teachers and for some colleagues, who were not quite sure where this initiative would take us. At first, some of our more established colleagues did not see the teacher-librarian role that was evolving as our new work; however, our teaching eventually became an anchor in itself, proving IL's and the librarians' place in the university curriculum beyond a doubt. The IL plan became a document we could share with the campus and others interested in establishing an IL program. We wanted the IL plan to provide an overview of the library's goals for this initiative, and of the work that we were doing to support student success in IL. Maintaining the plan as a living document has allowed us to annually review our direction and, equally important, to bring it up at planning meetings for the URI General Education Program. As an example, when other co-curricular or academic units thought they would consider dropping or asking for radical change in what the library offered their students, the IL plan provided an illustration so that they could also see that we valued and appreciated the interconnectedness of their unit's academic contributions as we sought to tie various programs outside the library into a web of resources for student success.

It was an enormous endeavor to write the IL plan; as we met and wrote, IL became our cause, and the plan became our manifesto and a pillar of our twenty-three-year experience with building an IL program. Over time, our library colleagues saw the benefit of the IL plan as a tool for planning, reflection, and public relations. The plan has always been both realistic and aspirational, sometimes loftier than we could attain. But it is my pleasure today to recognize that in 2022 we have accomplished the majority of our long-term goals.

A Note on Changes in Higher Education

Instruction coordinators are often required to write and review the reports necessary for regular accreditation by their institution's accrediting body. In recent times, many accrediting bodies in the United States required IL instruction to be provided by the college or university's library. As educational trends and philosophies change so too does the place of responsibility for IL in accreditation. In recent years, the requirement for IL has remained but is no longer the sole responsibility of the library. Changes that can upset or influence your IL program may come about on your campus due to administration or budget changes, or due to shifts in regional or national oversight, depending on your institution's organizational structure.

In New England, from 2000 to 2015, the standards for higher education included a specific Library Standard, requiring libraries to ensure the provision of IL. This standard boosted the value of our credit courses at URI as well as the value of the entire IL plan. The NEASC (now NECHE) Library Standard was removed from the standards in 2015; however, IL instruction is still expected and required by the Academic Program Standard (New England Commission of Higher Education [NECHE], 2021). The NECHE change is an example of how depending on only one anchor could have destabilized our IL program. Looking to several established local, regional, and national standards and organization values will help to sustain and anchor your overall program.

Culture of Assessment at URI

As our library IL program developed over the years, higher education, and URI, became more invested in an assessment process that is "committed to evidence-informed reflection and continual improvement, aligned with expectations from the URI's accrediting body, NECHE" (Office for the Advancement of Teaching and Learning, 2022). Assessment shows the impact of our teaching and provides direction in how to improve. From the beginning of our program, we used a variety of anonymous surveys, simple pre-tests and post-tests, formative, and summative assessments in our many teaching settings. These included one-shot instruction, programmatic IL for introductory writing, first-year orientation sessions, the Talent Development Program, and our credit bearing courses. For a few years, we even gave a final exam in the LIB 120 credit course that was adapted from the Bay Area Community College (BACC) Information Competency Proficiency Exam (Larsen et al., 2010). While our assessment efforts were useful, they were not uniform, thus making comparisons complicated. Some of this randomness is due to the lack of a formal library academic program, such as a major or minor program of study. Some of it is due to the big differences in the goals of each instruction program or initiative. If we were a larger staff, we might have an assessment librarian or a point person who could wrangle all of our assessment priorities and methods, but that was not the case.

In 2010, the university began working on yet another complete revision of the General Education Program that would bring it in line with our accrediting body and the national effort to assess student learning using learning outcomes. A library faculty colleague was a member of the General Education Revision Task Force (GERTF) where he was able to strongly advocate for including IL as a required learning outcome. The new General Education Program was designed as a four-year model employing twelve learning outcomes that would be the same for all university academic programs. As Head of Instruction and Information Literacy Librarian, I was invited to meet with GERTF to suggest models for achieving IL as one of those outcomes. I offered several models: scaffolding already existing programmatic IL across the four-year curriculum, having every student enroll in LIB 120, or inviting courses from across the curriculum to identify as IL courses. A few GERTF members found it difficult to grasp that it was necessary to "teach IL" more than once. They thought having a freshmen library orientation should take care of it. I compared learning to do research with learning other concepts (math, writing, foreign languages) that require continual practice and assessment to accomplish the learning. This analogy resonated and, ultimately, the third option was adopted.

The university was strengthening its assessment initiative and working on a homegrown framework based on rubrics created by teaching faculty. University staff and instructors were learning about assessment and beginning to learn the language of learning outcomes in readiness for the new General Education Program. Librarians had also quietly been working on developing an IL rubric that could be used to determine whether URI students were learning IL. We believed if we could measure IL on campus, faculty and administrators would be able to see the evidence and pay more attention to our efforts. Starting in 2008, a small group of us fiddled with a fledgling IL rubric. This first IL rubric did not garner any attention or support for awhile, and we floundered a bit; however, a serendipitous opportunity to share our teaching and assessment work with expert staff of the URI Office of Student Learning and Outcomes Assessment and Accreditation (SLOAA) Committee was just the kick-start we needed. Casual conversations with the director of SLOAA soon got us the attention and support of URI assessment staff who worked with us to develop and test a campus-wide IL rubric (Kinnie et al., 2013).

A multi-year project involved interested and motivated faculty from almost every college of the university. We introduced subject faculty to the AAC&U

Information Literacy VALUE Rubric as a starting point (n.d.). Through a series of workshops, faculty from six of our seven colleges tested the URI IL Rubric (based on the AAC&U) on authentic student work. In follow up meetings we discussed what the word research means in various disciplines as well as what evidence of student IL would look like to the faculty. The final iteration of the rubric was endorsed by URI Library faculty and by the URI Learning Outcomes Oversight Committee (LOOC), the faculty arm of SLOAA. Further, the IL Rubric was used as a model for the other eleven learning outcomes in the new General Education Program. A downside to this mostly positive outcome is that the rubric was designed before the ACRL *Framework*, so it is based on the ACRL *Standards* (ACRL, 2015; ACRL, 2000). Too much time and energy had been expended to start all over; though we do hope to have an opportunity to reshape the rubric when time allows. The upside to all of this is clear; having an IL plan and working with and across campus units to share the success of our work was gaining traction!

A panel of discipline experts was assigned for each of the twelve general education learning outcomes to review courses. Hundreds of courses, both previously part of the General Education Program and newly proposed courses, needed to be approved for acceptance to the new program. Two library colleagues and I were asked to be the review panel for the IL learning outcome. Using the rubric, we approved approximately sixty courses that applied for the IL designation (MacDonald et al., 2016). This was a challenging, exciting, and rewarding opportunity for all of us. We had a window into how IL would be incorporated into the courses, and often met with faculty proposers to discuss and tweak IL activities based on our knowledge of what might help their students most.

All of this happened at a very fortuitous time in academic library history. The ACRL was working on a complete reinterpretation of IL for higher education. The new model, the ACRL *Framework for Information Literacy for Higher Education* (ACRL, 2015) spoke directly to all of our teaching practice. During the summer of 2014, my colleagues and I developed and proposed a complete revision to our original LIB 120 course and submitted proposals for 2 new IL courses. This worked in our favor, showing support for the new General Education Program, which needed hundreds of IL student seats in dozens of courses to be successful. It also meant we could expand the IL content across three courses to focus on more detailed aspects of IL, which reflected more of *The Framework*. Approved in 2015, we now offer a sequence of three courses: LIB 150: Search Strategies for the Information Age, LIB 250: Research Across Disciplines, and LIB 350G: Current Issues of the Information Age. The courses are taught face-to-face, hybrid, and online in fall, spring, and summer semesters for approximately 250 students each academic year. Course instructors are Public Service Department faculty librarians. Teaching is now part of our regular negotiated workload.

When URI rolled out this model of general education in 2015, IL was finally recognized as an assessable and valuable learning content area. We went from "Information literacy? What's that?" in 1998 to becoming part of a required component of the general education curriculum in 2015. Readers may note that seventeen years is quite a long time to wait for this to happen. Consider the anchors mentioned earlier in this chapter, anchors that we used to get our program up and running and those that have kept it operational all these years. We depended on and pointed to foundational documents of the university, of higher education, and of academic librarianship, to show how IL serves students and the URI community in their quest to fulfill these foundational beliefs. We took time to learn the curriculum of General Education and of our liaison departments. Being appointed to faculty senate committees focused directly on the curriculum allowed us to advocate for IL from different vantage points. Being involved at this level, we learned the details of upcoming proposals, advocated for our interests, voiced opinions, and voted. We were directly involved in these decisions. While fulfilling our faculty service responsibilities, we continued to support and improve long-standing IL programs such as instruction for introductory writing courses, the Talent Development Program, and teaching one-shot subject instruction for our liaison areas, as well as teaching the LIB credit courses. We had also developed the habit of regularly reviewing the IL plan against the context of our institutional and higher education priorities. This enables us to continue to make adjustments to what and how we teach, and how we assess those efforts.

Letting Go?

With over 160 courses approved for the IL learning outcome, we have clearly shepherded IL into the curriculum (University of Rhode Island, n.d.b). Courses with the IL learning outcome come from the expected subject areas such as English, Writing, and History as well as the less expected, like Oceanography, Sustainable Agriculture, and Industrial Engineering. While we continue to teach three LIB credit courses, plus sessions for all introductory writing courses, the Talent Development Program, and other subject-specific courses, we recognized the fact that librarians alone cannot teach all the IL that would support the university's 17,000 students. We are confident that IL is being taught, practiced, and assessed within General Education. Faculty who teach courses with the IL outcomes in General Education know we are available for consultation. All general education outcomes are assessed on a revolving three-year assessment program, thus there are checks and balances for the IL-designated courses.

While we are currently faced with staff reductions due to retirements and a library administration with a focus on other initiatives, we are heartened that there is more awareness and teaching of IL than at any time prior on our campus. Reflecting on the ACRL *Characteristics of Programs of Information Literacy that Illustrate Best Practices: A Guideline*, I see where our work is strong and sustained, and also identify many areas that need attention. No educational program is ever completed, owing to the constant changes in the world of higher education and how they impact every facet of the university. What will the next general education program entail? What will the university's next strategic plan focus be?

These elements, and others, may sustain or derail our work, so we must be as ready and nimble as we can to keep our programs moving forward.

For now, we still have the capacity to teach the long-standing IL instruction programs at URI, but with so many students, some of our programs are in temporary jeopardy. In order to expand IL instruction beyond what we librarians can teach, and beyond the General Education Program—and to provide more support to non-library faculty in this endeavor—two librarians and one faculty developer from the office of the Advancement of Teaching and Learning have been offering a four-day high-impact teaching seminar, Researching Across the Disciplines (RAD) (Office for the Advancement of Teaching and Learning, n.d.). The RAD seminar has been completed by almost forty URI instructors further reaching thousands of students each year with IL. RAD provides an in-depth immersive experience for faculty to explore IL within their discipline and courses, and to share ideas with other faculty across the campus. Participants create action plans, which reflect changes they plan to make in their teaching, allowing students to practice important IL concepts and skills.

IL at Other Colleges and Universities

College and universities everywhere teach IL, whether it is well articulated and transparent or buried deep within the thousands of assigned papers, projects, and presentations done by students. What follows are a few examples of the different ways that academic libraries integrate IL into their school's curricula, using some of the same anchors that my colleagues and I did. Yet these librarians have applied them in a customized way for their academic needs and environment.

Keene State College, Keene, New Hampshire

Professor Elizabeth Dolinger of Keene State College (KSC) and her colleagues created a revolutionary IL overhaul in 2012 at Mason Library. Librarians knew that by using the one-shot instruction model they were limited to teaching IL skills with no time for students to experience and apply conceptual understanding of IL or the information landscape. Additionally, there was little chance for meaningful assessment. Further, the instruction was scatter-shot and uneven, dependent on faculty-librarian relationships, or just simple time limitations. These are common ailments for any IL instruction program and KSC librarians were ready for a major change. As a faculty they designed an academic minor in Information Studies, consisting of five courses and based on the ACRL *Framework*. Information Studies students could take one or all of the courses but completing all five earned the minor in Information Studies. Developing and implementing this program encompassed and fulfilled all aspects of the *Characteristics of Best Practices* document. With great disappointment, this program was closed in 2021 due to massive college budget cuts, and a general downsizing of the college. On a happier note, one Information Studies course remains as a general education course and may be required by several other academic majors. (E. Dolinger, personal communication, October 14, 2021).

Western Michigan University, Kalamazoo, Michigan

Professor Dianna Sachs of Western Michigan University (WMU) explains that Waldo Library librarians had for many years provided students with a well-known asynchronous online tutorial, *Research Path*. The library recently launched the *Information Literacy Microcourse*, which is a self-paced set of nine mix-and-match modules, each focused on a different IL concept. The course is asynchronous and built into the learning management system. All students are automatically enrolled and those who complete the modules earning a score of at least 80% on the final quiz receive a completion certificate that can be submitted to their professor. This initiative required an amazing amount of collaboration from many departments to be successful. The librarians had great support from their dean and associate deans, and the cooperation of the instructional designers and online instruction team. Additionally, IL is included in the WMU general education program for introductory writing and oral/digital communication courses. WMU librarians have achieved many of the *Characteristics of Best Practices in IL Programs* document with this initiative (D. Sachs, personal communication, October 19, 2021).

Salve Regina University, Newport, Rhode Island

At Salve Regina University's McKillop Library, Assistant Director Lisa Richter shared that a project to review course syllabi has been very fruitful due to the support from university administration that shared a multi-year collection of syllabi with the library in order to complete curriculum mapping process for Nursing with other departments next in line. Curriculum mapping can assist with planning and sequencing of instruction in order to reduce redundancy and utilize resources more wisely. Their plan is to reach students at important points in their academic majors, including key gateway, research methods, and senior capstone courses. This work happens due to intentional and positive faculty/librarian relationships. McKillop librarians also work closely with the Writing Center by co-teaching research and writing sessions. These elements create sustainable IL opportunities to the benefit of all students. (L. Richter, personal communication, October 22, 2021).

Tulsa Community College, Tulsa, Oklahoma

Lisa Haldeman, library director at Tulsa Community College's (TCC) Northeast Campus shared information about their IL program that has found success by collaborating with other units of this large community college, such as the TCC Institutional Research and Development department. With close to 25,000 students, support from multiple units help librarians to develop smart, savvy IL instruction that reaches many students in spite of a limited staff of librarians. In 2015, the community college librarians developed a college-wide assessment of the results of librarian-led IL instruction within the institution's Academic Strategies course. The results were definitely interesting, but the side effect of the project was that Academic Strategies instructors realized how vital this instruction is for their students. Three librarians were asked by Academic Strategies course leadership to develop an online IL module for all incoming TCC students (Brennan & Haldeman, 2018).

Reflection

Reflection is a powerful activity and writing this chapter has led me to a refreshed and revitalized understanding of the value of our work in the lives of students. Often, our work is concealed because, while we teach the concepts and skills that are the foundation of critical thinking, these concepts and skills are not always fully measured through assessment. Instruction coordinators everywhere teach, assess, and document the results of IL efforts; but what reach does your annual instruction report have? Numbers and anecdotes are well-known by those who craft the reports, but we must find more avenues for sharing our rewards.

Using the anchors available at each college or university and within higher education, we can more effectively share IL successes with committees, task forces, and administrators. We can demonstrate that our programs effectively teach critical thinking, close reading, and information research. Searching institutions for the documents, reports, and initiatives that may intersect with our own efforts can help open doors to conversation with institutional partners. At URI, two librarians published *Instruction@theURI Libraries* to share the good news about IL at URI (MacDonald & Izenstark, 2012–2017). Good news and good results attract more notice, and as instruction coordinator, you can use your voice to spread the word. We must continue to shine a light on the significant efforts and work of instruction librarians everywhere and raise the curtain to explore the many layers in the "mud of research" so that our students can continue to excel in in their own journeys of learning.

References

Association of American Colleges and Universities. (n.d.). *Information literacy VALUE rubric.* http://www.aacu.org/value/rubrics/information-literacy

American Association of School Librarians. (2000). Information literacy: A position paper.

American Library Association. (1989). *Presidential Committee on Information Literacy: Final report.* https://www.ala.org/acrl/publications/whitepapers/presidential

Association of College & Research Libraries. (2000). *Information literacy competency standards for higher education.* American Library Association. https://alair.ala.org/bitstream/handle/11213/7668/ACRL%20Information%20Literacy%20Competency%20Standards%20for%20Higher%20Education.pdf?sequence=1

Association of College & Research Libraries. (2019). *Characteristics of programs of information literacy that illustrate best practices: A guideline.* Instruction Section Website. https://acrl.ala.

org/IS/instruction-tools-resources-2/higher-education-environment/characteristics-of-programs-of-information-literacy-that-illustrate-best-practices-a-guideline/

Association of College and Research Libraries. (2015). *Framework for information literacy for higher education*. http://www.ala.org/acrl/standards/ilframework

Brennan, A., & Haldeman, L. (2018). Filling in the potholes: Providing smooth pathways for successful library instruction for first-year students. In K. Brown, D. Gilchrist, S. Goek, L.J. Hinchliffe, K. Malenfant, C. Ollis, & A. Payne (Eds.), *Shaping the campus conversation on student learning and experience: Activating the Results of Assessment in Action*. Association of College & Research Libraries.

Burkhardt, J.M., MacDonald, M., Rathemacher, A., Kelland, L., & Vocino, M. (2000). *Plan for information literacy at the University of Rhode Island* (ED 455849). ERIC. https://eric.ed.gov/?id=ED455849

Endorsement of mission statement for the University of Rhode Island. Faculty Senate Bills. Paper 1793. (2005). https://digitalcommons.uri.edu/facsen_bills/1793 https://digitalcommons.uri.edu/facsen_bills/1793

Kinnie, J., MacDonald, M., & Finan, E. (2013, May 2–4). *Measure by measure: Composing and rehearsing a campus-wide IL rubric* [Paper presentation]. LOEX. Nashville, TN. United States. https://digitalcommons.uri.edu/cgi/viewcontent.cgi?article=1012&context=lib_ps_pubs

Larsen, P., Izenstark, A., & Burkhardt, J. (2010). Aiming for assessment: Notes from the start of an information literacy course assessment. *Communications in Information Literacy*, 4(1), 61–70. 10.15760/comminfolit.2010.4.1.88

MacDonald, M.C., Kinnie, J., & Izenstark, A. (2016). Do faculty know "IL"?: Information literacy understandings and general education student learning outcomes. *LOEX Quarterly*, 43(2) https://commons.emich.edu/loexquarterly/vol43/iss2/3

MacDonald, M., & Izenstark, A. (2012–2017). Instruction @ the URI Libraries. https://digitalcommons.uri.edu/instructionnews/

New England Commission of Higher Education. (2021). Standards for accreditation. Standard four. https://www.neche.org/resources/standards-for-accreditation#standard_four

Office for the Advancement of Teaching and Learning. (2022). *Program assessment*. University of Rhode Island. https://web.uri.edu/atl/assessment/

Office for the Advancement of Teaching and Learning. (n.d.). *HIT seminar: Researching across the disciplines*. University of Rhode Island. https://web.uri.edu/atl/researching-across-the-disciplines-hit-seminar/

Shapiro, J.J., & Hughes, S.K. (1996). Information literacy as a liberal art. *Educom Review, 31*(2). https://www.educause.edu/apps/er/review/reviewArticles/31231.html

University Libraries. (1994). *Mission statement*. University of Rhode Island.

University Libraries. (1994). *Vision statement*. University of Rhode Island.

University of Rhode Island. (2007–2008). *2007–08 Catalog*. https://catalogarchives.uri.edu/catalog/archivedPDFs/catalog07_08.pdf

University of Rhode Island. (1996). *Mission statement*. University of Rhode Island.

University of Rhode Island. (n.d.a). *General education overview*. https://web.uri.edu/general-education/2021/02/26/general-education-assessment/

University of Rhode Island. (n.d.b). Rhode Island higher education facts. https://web.uri.edu/academic-planning/files/factslist.pdf

PART II
Moving and Growing Together

3

PROGRAM FOUNDATIONS: ESTABLISHING VALUES, BOUNDARIES, AND PRIORITIES

Rebecca Miller Waltz

Introduction

"Well, it really seems like the junk drawer of the library—you know, the place where projects and people go if there's not a better fit somewhere else." When I stepped into the head of Library Learning Services role at Penn State University Libraries, this was how a new colleague described the work of that department. The statement was a bit disturbing. At that moment in time, however, I could see that it was also accurate. Although teaching, learning, and information literacy were identified as library priorities, the purpose, mission, values, and priorities of the department and team focused on this work were unclear to many, including those who were part of the team. As an outsider coming in to work with and lead this team, I saw a group of individuals with much experience, expertise, and passion. What was missing was a shared vision that would leverage these strengths in a way that would support the team in growing in a specific direction together.

The *Characteristics of Programs of Information Literacy That Illustrate Best Practices: A Guideline* document articulates that instruction programs in academic libraries should have a defined program design with a clear statement of mission and structure (Association of College & Research Libraries [ACRL], 2019). While that sounds easy enough when reading these characteristics, the reality for most instruction programs and their leaders is much messier. University and library strategic priorities shift, people come and go, and traditional strategies and relationships compete and conflict with new ideas and innovations. It also is interesting to note that the first version of the *Characteristics of Programs of Information Literacy That Illustrate Best Practices: A Guideline* was approved in 2003, hot on the heels of the 2000 approval of the now-rescinded *Information Literacy Competency Standards for Higher Education* (ACRL, 2019; ACRL, 2000). The *Information Literacy Competency Standards for Higher Education* positioned libraries and librarians as active partners in the teaching

DOI: 10.4324/9781003038634-6

process and helped academic libraries succeed in truly engaging with their institutions' teaching missions in ways that they hadn't before (ACRL, 2000).

In 2016, with the approval of the *ACRL Framework for Information Literacy for Higher Education* (*The Framework*), the library instruction landscape shifted again as our profession began to build on what we had learned during the previous two decades (ACRL, 2015). Specifically, *The Framework* states that "librarians have a greater responsibility in identifying core areas within their own knowledge domain that can extend learning for students, in creating a new cohesive curriculum for information literacy, and in collaborating more extensively with faculty" (ACRL, 2015, para. 2). The practical implications of *The Framework* included libraries questioning their traditional models of instruction, such as one-shot instruction sessions, and experimenting with new ways of engaging students and supporting student success.

Let's go back to the teaching and learning department as junk drawer. Every academic library deals with instabilities. Is it any wonder, then, that library instruction programs, library instruction teams, or library teaching and learning departments might lose their way every now and then? More traditional librarian roles and teaching strategies might end up living alongside totally new roles and experimental strategies in a way that might not make sense and look a bit like a junk drawer. Times of transition can be messy and challenging but are also a given. While sometimes difficult to navigate, these times often present opportunities for change and growth within the organization. For library instruction programs, it falls to the leader to manage these transitions and ensure that their library instruction program establishes or re-establishes a firm foundation. This firm foundation consists of:

- a clear and shared understanding of the team and the work,
- clarity of each team member's individual role, and
- well-articulated team priorities and partnerships.

This chapter explores reasons and ways to engage with these three elements, each of which could easily be their own chapters in this book. Consider this chapter a primer and an introduction to establishing a firm foundation for your library instruction program.

Scoping the Team and the Work

The best place to start building a strong foundation for a library instruction program is with the people who are or who will be doing the work. I mentioned how the lack of a shared vision can contribute to confusion or misconceptions, from both inside and outside of a library instruction program and ultimately impede a program's success. Developing a shared vision asks team members to consider who they are as a team, how they define the teaching and learning work they are doing, and why this work ultimately matters. These can be challenging questions and difficult conversations; for leaders facilitating these types of discussions, building trust with and among the team and creating a safe environment is essential.

Trust and Safety

All teams comprise individuals who bring past experiences and understandings with them. Some teams who have worked together for a long time bring collective work experiences and understandings that new team members, including leaders, may need to take some time to appreciate. Other teams, who may be newly formed or created out of changing organizational structures or approaches, will have individuals from different contexts and perspectives coming together for the first time. Whatever place an instruction team is currently in will benefit from a leader's close attention to the individual and group experiences and backgrounds. As educators, we're all aware of the importance of considering our students' characteristics and needs, and this mental model translates well into leadership approaches. It's important for instruction program leaders to take the time to learn more about the team, as both individuals and a group, in order to create and sustain trust within that group.

The emerging discussion surrounding trauma-informed workplaces and leadership is relevant here, as we think about building trust and creating safe environments in which groups can engage in exciting and innovative work and individuals can flourish. 'Trauma' can mean a lot of different things, but Katharine Manning, author of a 2022 *Harvard Business Review* article on trauma-informed workplaces, defines trauma as "an emotional injury that affects performance and well-being" (para. 4). A recent *Chronicle of Higher Education* article also advocates for trauma-informed leadership, particularly for "wounded workgroups," which, let's face it, could be any of our teams, especially as we all struggle to cope with a pandemic and significant social and political turbulence (Vaillancourt, 2022). The bottom line? It's important to acknowledge what colleagues have experienced and to "focus your initial efforts on creating a work culture in which they finally feel seen and safe" (Vaillancourt, 2022, para. 16).

Similarly, all teams include existing power structures and likely reflect library and institutional systems of inequity, white supremacy and privilege, and oppression. Everyone on the team will have been affected, in some way, by these existing structures and systems. While it would be impossible for an instruction program leader to deal with these problematic structures and systems at the library or institutional level, they can absolutely deal with these at the team level. Talking about and addressing racism, privilege, and power can be very difficult, but is critical to creating a safe and inclusive team environment and to leveraging the diverse ideas and perspectives that are essential to innovative work. Racism, privilege, power, oppression, and inequity are elements of everyone's experiences and of our larger systems. Library instruction program leaders need to create space to acknowledge this and to collaboratively develop team norms, processes, and policies that reflect diversity, equity, inclusion, accessibility, and belonging. Both the team and the communities the team serves will benefit from this acknowledgment and collaborative actions. Instruction program leaders may not be trained in doing this type of work, but many resources exist for supporting these discussions; the "Diversity, Equity, and Inclusion" chapter in Elaina Norlin's *The Six-Step Guide to Library Worker Engagement* offers a good starting point (2021). Norlin (2021) details the role of this type of work in creating a healthy organizational foundation.

Acknowledging and building an understanding of trauma, racism, inequity, oppression, power, and privilege is critical to creating a safe and inclusive team environment built on trust. The same *Harvard Business Review* article mentioned earlier identifies psychological safety as the most critical factor in making a team function (Manning, 2022, para. 7). The Center for Creative Leadership defines psychological safety at work as "a shared belief by members of a team that others on the team will not embarrass, reject, or punish them for speaking up" (Leading Effectively Staff, 2022, para. 9). Along the same lines, Patrick Lencioni's (2002) leadership model, explained in *The Five Dysfunctions of a Team: A Leadership Fable,* identifies the absence of trust as a primary team dysfunction and underscores the role of trust as a team foundation.

It is important to acknowledge that some library instruction program leaders will be better positioned and supported than others to create a trauma-informed, inclusive, and psychologically safe space for their teams to do the hard work they need to do. As Veronica Arellano Douglas and Joanna Gadsby (2019) point out, nonsupervising instruction coordinators face very real challenges when it comes to "creating team," one of the categories of relational practice identified in their article on library instruction coordination (para. 33). The work it takes to build a team based on trust and construct a safe and inclusive environment is often "taken for granted or ignored," despite the significance of this work (Douglas & Gadsby, 2019, para. 33). While it certainly can feel demoralizing when this work isn't recognized, prioritized, or rewarded, know that it is indeed critical. Our organizations need to do better at recognizing and appreciating the efforts that go into this work. If we instruction program coordinators have the inclination and opportunity to move into higher level leadership roles, let's remember that and affirm the importance of this work throughout our organizations when we are in positions to do so.

If you take away one thought from this section, let it be this: put people first. This simple leadership goal, identified in another recent *Chronicle of Higher Education* article about trauma-informed leadership, will go a long way toward creating a caring environment for a team that will ultimately be creating and managing an instruction program reflecting the same principles of care, equity, safety, and belonging (Whitaker, 2020, para. 4). With this spirit of person-centered leadership and a focus on building trust, let's talk a bit more about who the instruction team really is.

Who Are We?

"Who are we?" is often a complicated question when it comes to library instruction programs. As noted earlier, some library instruction programs are facilitated by departments devoted to teaching and learning while others have a looser structure, with individuals from multiple departments and with different supervisors, supporting the library instruction program. As this chapter discussed earlier, it is important to acknowledge the type of library instruction program you are leading and identify appropriate strategies and approaches based on that. It might sound simple but taking some time to analyze what type of team you are leading and who the team members are will go a long way toward creating a strong program foundation. Later, we will discuss individual roles on the instruction team and the importance of shaping and supporting these roles, but for now let's focus on the big picture of the team and identifying a clear scope of work for that team.

Clarity around the scope of work and clear definition of the boundaries of the program is essential to a strong instruction program. As the *ACRL Characteristics of Programs of Information Literacy That Illustrate Best Practices: A Guideline* articulates, an instruction program is more than a group of activities that somehow fall into the category of "instruction" (ACRL, 2019). A true program is intentional, strategic, and bounded in order to enable and empower the instruction team and its leader to invest time, resources, and energy in the right places and ensure capacity for high-quality work and new ideas. Decisions about program boundaries need to be made based on a team's values, mission, vision, and goals, but it can be hard to separate out all of these strategic pieces when the work is ongoing and instruction requests are regularly rolling in.

A good starting point for creating program boundaries and organizing the "junk drawer" is creating an inventory of all the work and activities in which team members are actively engaged. This process can be as simple as having each team member develop and share a list of everything they are doing in order to create a comprehensive record of the individual team members' commitments. This activity will likely be eye-opening for the team, because the breadth and diversity of activities associated with teaching and learning can be astonishing. Next, the team can start to identify themes or categories that they see in the team inventory. As those categories emerge, a portrait of a team's portfolio also begins to emerge, and the team can begin to collaboratively mark boundary lines for their program. When I first joined the Library Learning Services team at Penn State University Libraries in 2015, we used this process to identify four main categories of work that ultimately created our program boundaries: teaching and learning expertise; foundational-level information literacy instruction; programming for outreach and student engagement; and coordination of library classrooms and learning spaces. By creating these boundaries, we had a better sense of what our team was working toward as well as what we could stop doing. We were able to use these categories of work to communicate with colleagues and administrators to justify team decisions and resource investments.

Creating categories of work and program boundaries alone still doesn't create the strong program foundation necessary for carrying instruction programs, leaders, and colleagues through times of change and transition. An instruction team's identity, like the instruction program itself, is more than its activities. To really dig into its identity and direction, the team will need to engage in further work that asks, "What are we doing?" and, "Why are we doing it?"

What Are We Doing?

The question, "What are we doing?" looks beyond individual activities and categories of a team's activities and asks the team to consider the purpose of their work and the instruction program, in general. These conversations may require more planning and facilitation, as the goal of these conversations is to support the team in developing a shared mission and vision that will guide their work and future decisions about projects, initiatives, and the team's scope of work. Facilitating these types of discussions is where instruction program leaders can rely on their skills and expertise as educators. As teachers, we rely on our ability to facilitate discussions and engineer collaborative learning experiences in the classroom. While our team members are absolutely not our students, our teacher toolbox can come in handy when planning conversations that will rely on the full participation and engagement of team members. This is where we can get creative and have fun with our teams.

While the words mission and vision are often used interchangeably, they do signify separate and important pieces of a strategic approach. According to the *Harvard Business Review*, a vision statement is aspirational, and a mission statement clearly defines a group's work (Kenny, 2014). So, in other words, "What are we doing?" and, "What do we want to be?" Many businesses have mission and vision statements to guide their work, and your institution probably does, as well. In developing the instruction team's mission and vision, look for areas of connection and alignment with the library's and institution's statements. The ACRL *Characteristics of Programs of Information Literacy That Illustrate Best Practices: A Guideline* articulates a number of recommendations for a library instruction program's mission, goals, and objectives, including a connection with institutional mission and goals and underscoring the importance of information literacy for our students (ACRL, 2019).

As an example of what this looks like in practice at Penn State University Libraries, the Library Learning Services team used their scope of work, ACRL guidelines and definitions, and the Penn State (2022) and Penn State University Libraries (2022) mission statements to write the following mission statement for guiding the team's work and communicate its goals:

> *Library Learning Services fosters foundational learning experiences and leads within the Libraries through innovative instructional practices. We cultivate informed scholars who are able to gather and evaluate information and to use information resources in meaningful ways throughout their academic careers and beyond.*
>
> (Library Learning Services, 2022)

Creating a shared mission and vision for an instruction program doesn't have to be a dreary exercise in wordsmithing. Quite the opposite: these activities should be creative and leverage each team member's passions and insights. While the inventory of activities and examples of mission and vision statements can help the group get started, consider ways to really push the team to think about their work in new ways. In *The Surprising Power of Liberating Structures: Simple Rules to Unleash a Culture of Innovation*, Henri Lipmanowicz and Keith McCandless (2014) offer up simple techniques to support exactly this type of work. This resource includes many exercises like the "Nine Whys," a conversation structure for teams to help them reach the fundamental purpose of their work, and "Appreciative Interviews," a process for identifying strengths and successes. Another personal favorite resource is the *75 Tools for Creative Thinking,* a card deck full of fun activities to support inventive and collaborative team thinking (http://75toolsforcreativethinking.com/).

Many resources exist for helping teams craft mission and vision statements to guide and direct their work, but there's another component teams need to consider as they think about their work: "Why are we doing it?"

Why Are We Doing It?

It's no secret that many library workers approach their work with passion and clear dedication to their own, personal values. Indeed, many library workers choose to work in libraries because their personal values align with the core values of librarianship: access, confidentiality and privacy, democracy, diversity, education and lifelong learning, intellectual freedom, the public good, preservation, professionalism, service, social responsibility, and sustainability (American Library Association [ALA], 2019). However, in her 2018 article introducing the world to the concept of vocational awe, Fobazi Ettarh explores the caution with which we should approach thinking and talking about our work in libraries in terms of passion, devotion, and awe. This is important to keep in mind when we talk about the values that we bring to and enact through our work; when teams talk about personal and group values, it can be easy to slip into a mode of romanticizing or idealizing our work. While our work is important—we wouldn't have chosen to do it if it we didn't think it was worthwhile—instruction program leaders need to help the team maintain perspective on their work in order to sustain morale, well-being, and healthy work-life approaches within their work environment.

With that disclaimer, let's return to talking about values that guide a team's or organization's work. At Penn State University Libraries, we think about values as "how we conduct ourselves and how we want to be treated by others … values serve as a 'lens' through which we, with our users, set priorities and make resource allocations" (*Values,* 2022). Similar to the American Library Association's set of core values, Penn State University Libraries' core values are: equity of access, diversity and inclusion, ethics and integrity, sustainability, empathy, and organizational excellence (Penn State University Libraries *Values,* 2022). The *Harvard*

Business Review offers a slightly different perspective on values, describing values as "the desired culture" of a business or a "behavioral compass" (Kenny, 2014, para. 5). The same article offers the example of Coca-Cola's values, which include the courage to shape a better future, leveraging collective genius, being real, and being accountable and committed. On its website, The Coca-Cola Company (2022) lists several additional core values: diversity, equity, and inclusion; equality, human and workplace rights; and supplier diversity.

Using the metaphor of values as a lens or a compass can be helpful for teams as they think through what matters to them in their work and how that can help guide decisions about time, roles, commitments, and resources. Coming up with a set of core values can feel daunting, but a 2018 *Harvard Business Review* article lays out a very simple process: give colleagues the opportunity to reflect and contribute thoughtfully, inventory and organize all ideas, identify a shortlist of values, discuss how everyone interprets the values, and develop a plan for integrating the values (Friedman). If this process sounds familiar, it's because this is very similar to what we've discussed for creating a scope of work and mission and vision statements! Each of these processes relies on team members feeling safe enough to share their ideas, having the capacity and space to reflect and contribute meaningfully, and working together to come to a consensus and shared understanding of who the library instruction team is, what the work is that they'll be doing, and why they are doing it.

There are some fun instruments and tools that library instruction program leaders can use to help colleagues articulate and communicate their own strengths and values. The *StrengthsFinder 2.0* tool is a commonly used online assessment for helping people identify their natural strengths, talents, and values (Gallup, 2022). The Library Learning Services team at Penn State used this tool to identify individual and group strengths and values. This group learning process led to a better understanding of team members' perspectives and affinities. Unfortunately, the *StrengthsFinder 2.0* tool is proprietary, which means that the tool must be licensed. An alternative tool is the *Life Values Inventory*, which is a freely accessible tool that can help individuals and organizations "clarify their values" (Life Values Inventory, 2021). Both the *StrengthsFinder 2.0* and the *Life Values Inventory* tools can support teams as they work to discover their individual and group *why*, and both include guides and resources for leveraging the insights that result from these assessments.

The process of discovering a team's values, mission, goals, and activities is not unlike the research process, in that it really isn't linear, can be very messy, and should be highly iterative. Ideally, a team's mission, goals, and activities would be directed by its values, but it can be challenging for a team, particularly a new team, to dive directly into a big brainstorming session around core values and principles. It might be easier to start conversations related to scoping a team and its work by looking at a team's current activities, which is why the question, "Who are we?" is posed first in this section. However, most teams will want to revisit their scope of work and program boundaries after, or as, they clarify their mission, vision, and values.

We've spent a lot of time talking about building a library instruction team and program; next, let's devote some time to exploring the importance of individual roles as part of the library instruction team and program. As teams think about the scope of work, mission, vision, and values for an instruction program, it's just as essential to consider the unique role that each individual team member plays in supporting and advancing these. This includes, but certainly is not limited to, the role of the instruction team leader. Each team member has a specific role to serve on the team, and clarifying, supporting, and intentionally evolving these roles is a significant instruction team leader responsibility.

Scoping Individual Roles

Literature from librarianship and beyond clearly links role clarity in workgroups with individual job satisfaction, success and happiness, and team productivity (Hassan, 2013; McCormack, 2014). More recently, research on the topic of low morale and job-related stress has identified unclear job expectations as one of the main causes of burnout (Mayo Clinic, 2021). Library instruction team leaders who want to help their teams and team members achieve positive outcomes and avoid harmful ones need to help each colleague understand their role on the team, explain expectations for that role, and offer resources and support for meeting those expectations.

Defining and Communicating Roles

As you think about the library instruction team and the roles of the individuals that comprise the team, we revisit the question, "Who are we?" This time, however, the focus will be on each individual team member, rather than the entire team. Each person on the team has a specific role to play, which should be clear to both the individual and the rest of the team. At first, the most clearly defined role on the team may be that of the leader or coordinator. According to the ACRL *Roles and Strengths of Teaching Librarians* document, coordinators lead instruction programs through project management, communication skills, vision, collaboration, and assessment, and should be prepared to navigate complex and changing environments (ACRL, 2017). These areas of responsibility look different at every institution and every library, so having a well-scoped coordinator role description can be key for ensuring that everyone knows what to expect of the person in this role, including the coordinator themselves! It can be helpful for instruction program leaders and their supervisors to outline expectations, tasks, and goals for the coordinator role, and to clearly communicate this with the rest of the team and the rest of the organization.

Similarly, each person on the team needs to know what their role is, what the expectations for that role are, and what support they have for meeting those expectations. Instruction program leaders should start by meeting with each team member individually and discussing their responsibilities, workload, interests, and goals, and use this to align team members with the defined scope of work for the instruction program. Group discussions should follow individual discussions in order to ensure that team members know what to expect from each other and can begin to consider how their roles work together. Documenting the individual roles that emerge from these discussions is important and can help communicate about these roles with colleagues outside of the library instruction team, as well. This documentation can be as formal as an official job description or as informal as a list of bullet points communicating an individual's main tasks, responsibilities, or commitments.

For additional role clarity, consider who may be the point person or lead on particular areas of the library instruction program, and the projects and tasks that may be associated with that. A personal favorite tool for this sort of documentation is a RACI chart, which denotes who is Responsible, Accountable, Consulted, and Informed about particular areas of work or for different projects, as indicated in Figure 3.1. In a RACI chart, these words describe specific roles: the people who are *responsible* are actually doing the work, the people who are *accountable* are the ones assigning and approving the work, the people who are *consulted* share feedback and input, and the people who are *informed* are kept up to date on the project or area of work.

Project: Creating an academic integrity tutorial:	Library instruction program leader	Instruction librarian(s)	Library instructional designer	Outreach coordinator	Student interns
Assesses learner needs	A	R	C	I	C
Identifies learning outcomes and designs learning experience	A	C	R	I	C
Develops the tutorial	A	C	R	I	I
Collaborates with information technology colleagues to publish tutorial to web	A	I	R	C	I
Communicates with partners about tutorial	A	R	I	R	C
Assesses impact of tutorial	A	R	R	I	C

FIGURE 3.1 Sample RACI chart

RACI charts are common project management tools, and templates abound on the Web. Whether or not you end up using a tool like a RACI chart, having clarifying conversations with each team member about their individual roles can ultimately help the entire team be more successful.

Establishing role clarity for team members can be one of the most difficult things library instruction program leaders end up doing, particularly when they may not have total control over their colleagues' workloads or other responsibilities. Furthermore, individual roles are constantly shifting and changing, often in response to institutional directions or new trends. For this reason, library instruction program leaders must collaborate closely with team members to proactively evolve their roles in order to support the overall mission and goals of the instruction program.

Role Evolution

Library instruction program and team leaders endeavoring to build truly dynamic information literacy programs need to stay abreast of trends in higher education and libraries and of their communities' needs so they can purposefully direct their instruction programs and their teams. Documents like the ACRL *Roles and Strengths of Teaching Librarians* illustrate the established core strengths and roles associated with librarians who teach, but other annual publications, such as the report from the ACRL Research Planning and Review Committee and the *EDUCAUSE Horizon Reports* (https://library.educause.edu/resources/2021/2/horizon-reports), consider current and future developments that will impact academic libraries and higher education (ACRL, 2017; 2021-22 ACRL Research Planning & Review Committee [ACRL Research], 2022). Library instruction program leaders need to pay attention to these trends and themes to ensure that their programs and their teams are proactively working toward meeting the needs of the broader institution and community of students.

Just as our understanding of information literacy and library instruction have shifted over the past few decades, the roles of the individuals who do this work have also shifted and will continue to do so. Library instruction program leaders must look forward and help their team members explore new areas of expertise and new areas of focus. Even the 'bread and butter' areas of an instruction librarian's job, such as teaching library workshops or facilitating research consultations, can evolve and be influenced by new pedagogies, new knowledge about how people learn, or broader social changes, such as a global pandemic. This balancing act of viewing traditional library roles through new lenses and frameworks requires library instruction program leaders to bring intention and creativity to the work of scoping and supporting individual team members' roles. Again, staying abreast of current and future trends and themes is a good place to start.

Examples of current trends and themes include a renewed focus on online learning, microcredentials, accessibility, open educational resources, artificial intelligence, learning analytics, and new ways of thinking about student engagement and student success, among others (ACRL Research, 2022; Pelletier, et al., 2022). Not all new trends and themes will be appropriate or relevant for all library instruction programs, so it is important for library instruction program leaders to maintain an institutional awareness in order to be able to identify the specific areas of expertise and knowledge that the team will need to stay relevant and be leaders within the library and the institution. It's exciting to think about the ways that individual roles can shift, expand, and evolve with the ultimate goal of better supporting our students and our communities. However, it can also feel overwhelming and daunting, particularly in moments of great change. Library instruction program leaders play an essential role in managing this tension for their teams; they need to approach the evolution of individual roles and program directions with collaboration, empathy, and intention. Helping colleagues tap into new areas of interest and expertise, and perhaps also letting go of responsibilities that are no longer inspiring them or serving the program, can be one of the best parts of instruction program leadership.

Continued Learning and Succession Planning

Continued learning is an essential element for all library instruction team members, including the leader, as they work toward building a program that is both responsive to community need and forward-looking. Library instruction team members need opportunities and space to engage with new ideas and trends. This continued learning can and should happen in many different ways: through mentorships, formal learning opportunities like classes or conferences, informal reading and discussion groups, and communities of practice, among others. As library instruction program leaders work with members of their team to scope individual roles and intentionally evolve these roles, creating professional development or continued learning plans can be helpful. Like creating a lesson plan, good professional development plans start with outcomes, include indicators of success, and identify resources and strategies that align with environmental affordances and constraints. If environmental constraints include budget constraints, library instruction program leaders might be encouraged to seek internal or external grant opportunities to aid in supporting individual and team growth in strategic ways. Ideally, these plans would be created and implemented on a regular timeline and potentially aligned with performance review processes. Even if your situation isn't ideal, you can still approach individual learning and growth with intention and vision.

A very specific piece of continued learning and library instruction program development is succession planning. In their succession planning toolkit, the University of Washington (2016) defines succession planning as identifying "future staffing needs and the people with the skills and potential to perform in these future roles" (p. 1). In other words, we need to ensure that critical positions, skills, and institutional knowledge is preserved and shared with others so that a library instruction program can remain strong and dynamic as team members, library leaders, and institutional collaborators come and go. Change may be the one constant in higher education, and we want to celebrate colleagues who choose new opportunities elsewhere or grow out of their current roles. It can be sad to lose a valued team member, but succession planning can help guarantee that a program will continue to thrive. Succession planning can also help other team members learn, grow, and identify future career directions. The University of Washington (2016) *Succession Planning Toolkit* identifies three main steps for succession planning: assessing, evaluating, and developing. Assessing is about identifying critical positions and skillsets, and evaluation is about considering who may be able to fill critical positions and the areas in which they would need to grow in order to fill those roles. Developing entails documenting knowledge and using that to develop individuals to be able to step into critical roles when needed. Library instruction program leaders may not need to develop a formal succession plan, but they should consider ways to start documenting needs and knowledge and developing team members. Then, when someone leaves the library instruction team for a new role or takes time for family leave, everyone will be prepared.

As we think about what individuals on our teams need to succeed and feel good about their work, we can look to models of academic motivation for additional understanding. Many of these models, such as John Keller's ARCS Model and Brett Jones's MUSIC model, emphasize elements associated with successful learning: the learner's agency in the learning process, the learner's confidence that they can succeed, and the learner's belief that others in their learning environment care about their success and about them as a person (Keller, 2010; Jones, 2022). These can also be fundamental elements for our colleagues who are individually and collaboratively learning and growing in a professional environment. As instruction program leaders, we need to consider how we can integrate these elements of agency, confidence, and care into our leadership (Waltz, 2021).

At this point, we've talked a lot about developing a team and individual roles within that team. While library instruction program leaders direct this work, they are also working with the team to plan the team's work, prioritize projects and partnerships, and ultimately implement the team's goals. As I noted, this work is iterative; as the team develops a strategic plan and identifies priorities, the team and individual scopes of work may shift a bit, as this is where big ideas move into the realm of reality.

Planning, Prioritizing, and Partnering

A library instruction program's priorities and partners signify where their resources, time, attention, and energy are invested. The library instruction team's priorities and partners need to be clearly defined and regularly assessed to ensure that the team's workload, investments, and directions are appropriate, relevant, and meaningful. New potential priorities and partners constantly present themselves, and library instruction programs with roadmaps of priorities and partners will be better prepared for making difficult decisions in these areas and for sustaining good relationships with institutional partners and administrators—even when a library instruction program leader has to decline an opportunity or say "no."

Priorities and Strategic Planning

Earlier in this chapter, we discussed program boundaries and categories of work for library instruction teams and programs. Establishing priorities is different, since this requires library instruction program leaders and team members to drill down into these categories of work and identify the specific projects, tasks, and responsibilities to which team members will commit. Establishing priorities also means determining which projects or tasks may be most important. Library instruction program leaders and their teams may have to make difficult decisions about which projects to support as resources and personnel shift. Having a clear set of priorities can help them make these decisions as well as clearly communicate these decisions beyond the team.

Just as the library instruction team's mission ought to align with that of the library and institution, the instruction program's programmatic priorities should support existing institutional strategic plans. If these plans directly address teaching or information literacy, these elements will be important to include in the library instruction program-level plan. The program-level plan, though, should reflect these larger institutional and library priorities, but also clarify this work in language and goals that make sense at the program level. Many resources exist for supporting strategic planning processes, such as the 2019 *Strategic Planning for Academic Libraries: A Step-by-Step Guide,* but the process doesn't have to be overly complicated or intense (Thompson et al.). Rather, this is where the team will build on the work they have already done on their scope, mission, and values. If the team can identify short-term and long-term goals that advance the scope, mission, and values of the team, along with the specific steps that will help them achieve those goals, that's your strategic plan. Like everything else discussed in this chapter, strategic plans and priorities will shift and evolve, and team leaders need to be prepared to keep these documents as timely and relevant as possible. Planning for annual, or even more frequent, reviews of strategic plans and priorities is a good way to keep these documents fresh but also keep them at the forefront of team members' minds. A good strategic plan is one that is simple and resonant enough that everyone can remember and act on it, even when it's not directly in front of them.

Every library instruction program leader understands that no goals can be met, or priorities achieved, without some level of collaboration. The library instruction program's strategic plan needs to include a clear list of partners and collaborators inside of and beyond the library, since none of our work is done in a vacuum or without the support and cooperation of others.

Partners and Collaborators in the Library

Earlier in this chapter, we discussed creating boundaries for library instruction programs. While this work is important for clarifying and supporting a team's work, boundaries also can sometimes be interpreted as territories. This interpretation can be detrimental to a library instruction program's ability to collaborate with library colleagues. Within the library, there are likely others who are doing work related to teaching, learning, outreach, and student engagement, but who are not members of the library instruction team. Subject or liaison librarians are primary examples of these colleagues, but roles focused on scholarly communications or research data management also often include teaching responsibilities and may not be considered part of core library instruction teams. Depending on your library's organizational structure and the size of your library, you may have more or fewer of these colleagues whose work boundaries overlap with your library instruction program's boundaries. Regardless, it's important to identify these potential areas of overlap and address them directly before program and job boundaries turn into fiercely protected territories. Library instruction program leaders need to be aware of the work that others are doing and try to understand organizational history and culture. This can be particularly important for leaders who may be joining a new organization or stepping onto a new team, but it's never too late to take a moment to better understand an organization's culture.

Clear communication with colleagues who may be doing similar work can lead to a healthy understanding of program boundaries and identification of potential partnerships that advance each unit's goals and priorities. As an example of what this can look like, "Expert Teams in the Academic Library: Going Beyond Subject Expertise to Create Scaffolded Instruction," focuses on the collaboration of two members of a core Penn State Libraries instruction team, an assessment expert, and a subject liaison working together to create a stronger discipline-based information literacy program (Wissinger et al., 2018). Overall, it is in everyone's best interest when library instruction program leaders bring an awareness and appreciation of others' expertise and intentionally identify areas where the library instruction team's expertise can combine with other areas of knowledge to better support our students and broader community.

Library colleagues who work in administration and fundraising are also important collaborators for library instruction programs. For the purposes of this chapter, I am defining roles related to executive leadership, financial services, and human resources as "administrative." Colleagues in administrative roles and fundraising roles may not immediately come to mind as important collaborators for library instruction programs, but these roles can be critical to supporting the health and growth of the library instruction program and team. Understanding administrative structures, budget processes, and human resources policies is essential knowledge for library instruction team leaders, and colleagues with expertise in these areas offer the most direct access to this knowledge. Making connections with these colleagues and nurturing these relationships will lead to better planning, leadership, and resource management. Similarly, proactively reaching out to individuals in library or institutional fundraising can help these individuals better understand the work of the library instruction team and ultimately connect donors and donations with areas of interest and need in the library instruction program. Library leadership, finances, human resources, and fundraising all represent areas of deep expertise held by library colleagues—reach out to these colleagues and see what you can learn from each other!

It takes many library colleagues to create and sustain a successful library instruction program, and the library instruction program leader plays an important role in setting the tone for and managing these relationships. However, these aren't the only collaborations and partnerships essential to a library instruction program's success. Next, let's think about how to take a strategic approach to cultivating and curating partnerships beyond the library.

Partners and Collaborators Beyond the Library

Beyond the library, there are likely many departments, programs, and leaders who are eager to partner with the library. Successful library instruction programs bring a proactive and strategic approach to identifying and collaborating with these external partners, rather than being reactive and waiting until a potential collaborator approaches the library instruction program.

Traditional external partners for library instruction programs include composition, rhetoric, and writing programs, first-year programs, general education programs, and student affairs units. These instructional partnerships often make sense, since the curricula for these programs need the information literacy expertise that library instruction programs are able to provide. However, these traditional partnerships need to be balanced with other institutional partnerships that may offer new ways for library instruction programs to support learners' needs and equitable outcomes for students. Library instruction program leaders can use their understanding of institutional strategic plans and priorities to identify offices, programs, and units that may better integrate library resources and expertise.

At Penn State, new partnerships with the Student Engagement Network, Global Engagement Network, Student Success Center, Student Disability Resources, and Office of Educational Equity have created opportunities for the library instruction program to partner with faculty and support student success. We identified these partnerships by using our mission, values, and understanding of institutional priorities to reconsider how we wanted to impact students. These new collaborations meant that we needed to spend less time and energy on our more traditional partnerships; for example, we adjusted our instructional modes in order to spend less face-to-face time in general education classes and spend more face-to-face time in other student engagement opportunities.

In general, partnerships within and beyond the library need to reflect the priorities, scope of work, mission, and values of the library instruction program and team. Partnerships and collaborations can be avenues to success, but they are also investments. Partnerships need to be regularly evaluated in terms of the investments the library instruction team is making in them and the resulting student and institutional impacts.

Final Thoughts

The work described in this chapter is hard. What can make it even more difficult is the understanding that this work must be sustained and ongoing. While there may be sweet spots in time where a team is fully staffed, well resourced, and synchronized in their efforts, most teams and programs are always going through some sort of transition or change. Maintaining relationships, reviewing progress, and monitoring priorities are constant concerns of a library instruction program leader, and it can be challenging to remember this when you're in the middle of the day-to-day work of the program.

Much of this chapter has been about looking forward while acknowledging and sometimes breaking with the past, on a number of different levels. At the program level, this work can become easier – or at least more comfortable – if it is integrated into the regular life of the team and the program. Instead of waiting for a crisis or "junk drawer" moment that exposes cracks or other issues with a program's foundation, library instruction program leaders need to review and reinforce that foundation collaboratively and consistently. This will likely require a cultural shift toward making the time and space for regular reflection and renewal, and will ultimately better position the library instruction program and those who support it.

Again, the work discussed in this chapter is hard. While rewarding and often motivating, leadership is also tough and can be isolating. Because of this, it's important for library instruction program leaders to carve out the space, time, relationships, and peer support that they need to sustain energy, passion, and morale. Leaders are pulled in many different directions during the day, and often have calendars full of teaching and meetings. If possible, library instruction program leaders need to be intentional about carving out time for individual reflection and peer connection. Block off time each week to think about what's going on: you can journal, catch up on new articles, or work on your own scholarship. Seek out people at other institutions doing similar work. If you don't have a peer network, reach out to some of the authors who have written chapters for this book—we'd love to hear from you!

In general, take care of yourself and prioritize your own health, safety, growth, and development, just as you would for your team members. The work that you're doing is challenging, but worth it.

References

2021-22 ACRL Research Planning & Review Committee. (2022). Top trends in academic libraries. *College & Research Libraries News, 83*(6), 243. 10.5860/crln.83.6.243

Association of College and Research Libraries. (2000). *Information literacy competency standards for higher education*. Association of College and Research Libraries.

Association of College & Research Libraries. (2015). *Framework for information literacy for higher education*. https://www.ala.org/acrl/standards/ilframework

Association of College & Research Libraries. (2017). *Roles and strengths of teaching librarians*. https://www.ala.org/acrl/standards/teachinglibrarians

Association of College & Research Libraries. (2019). *Characteristics of programs of information literacy that illustrate best practices: A guideline*. https://www.ala.org/acrl/standards/characteristics

American Library Association. (2019). *Core values of librarianship*. https://www.ala.org/advocacy/intfreedom/corevalues

The Coca-Cola Company. (2022). *Core values*. https://www.coca-colacompany.com/social-impact/people-values

Douglas, V.A., & Gadsby, J. (2019, July 10). All carrots, no sticks: Relational practice and library instruction coordination. *In the Library with the Lead Pipe*. http://www.inthelibrarywiththeleadpipe.org/2019/all-carrots-no-sticks-relational-practice-and-library-instruction-coordination/

Ettarh, F. (2018, January 10). Vocational awe and librarianship: The lies we tell ourselves. *In the Library with the Lead Pipe*. https://www.inthelibrarywiththeleadpipe.org/2018/vocational-awe/

Friedman, A. (2018, April 13). How to establish values on a small team. *Harvard Business Review*. https://hbr.org/2018/04/how-to-establish-values-on-a-small-team

Gallup. (2022). *CliftonStrengths*. https://www.gallup.com/cliftonstrengths/en/252137/home.aspx

Hassan, S. (2013). The importance of role clarification in workgroups: Effects on perceived role clarity, work satisfaction, and turnover rates. *Public Administration Review*, *73*(5), 716–725. 10.1111/puar.12100

Jones, B. (2022). *MUSIC model of motivation*. https://cmx.tpu.mybluehost.me/Music_Model/

Keller, J. (2010). *Motivational design for learning and performance: The ARCS Model approach*. Springer.

Kenny, G. (2014, September 3). Your company's purpose is not its mission, vision, or values. *Harvard Business Review*. https://hbr.org/2014/09/your-companys-purpose-is-not-its-vision-mission-or-values

Leading Effectively Staff. (2022, January 15). *What is psychological safety at work? Why a psychologically safe work environment matters & how to foster it*. Center for Creative Leadership. https://www.ccl.org/articles/leading-effectively-articles/what-is-psychological-safety-at-work/

Lencioni, P.M. (2002). *Five dysfunctions of a team: A leadership fable*. Jossey-Bass.

Library Learning Services. (2022). *Library Learning Services*. Penn State University Libraries. https://libraries.psu.edu/about/departments/library-learning-services

Life Values Inventory. (2021). *Life Values Inventory*. https://www.lifevaluesinventory.org/

Lipmanowicz, H., & McCandless, K. (2014). *The surprising power of liberating structures: Simple rules to unleash a culture of innovation*. Liberating Structures Press.

Manning, K. (2022, March 31). We need trauma-informed workplaces. *Harvard Business Review*. https://hbr.org/2022/03/we-need-trauma-informed-workplaces

McCormack, N. (2014). Managers, stress, and the prevention of burnout in the library workplace. *Advances in Librarianship*, *38*, 211–244. 10.1108/S0065-283020140000038008

Mayo Clinic Staff. (2021, June 5). Job burnout: How to spot it and take action. *Mayo Clinic*. https://www.mayoclinic.org/healthy-lifestyle/adult-health/in-depth/burnout/art-20046642

Norlin, E. (2021). *The six-step guide to library worker engagement*. ALA Editions.

Pelletier, K., McCormack, M., Reeves, J., Robert, J., Arbino, N., Al-Freih, M., Dickson-Deane, C., Guevara, C., Koster, L., Sanchez-Mendiola, M., Bessette, L.S., & Stine, J. (2022). *2022*

EDUCAUSE Horizon report: Teaching and learning edition. EDUCAUSE. https://library. educause.edu/resources/2022/4/2022-educause-horizon-report-teaching-and-learning-edition

Penn State. (2022). *Mission and values.* https://www.psu.edu/this-is-penn-state/mission-and-values/

Penn State University Libraries. (2022). *Organization at a glance.* https://libraries.psu.edu/about/organization-glance

Penn State University Libraries. (2022). *Values.* https://libraries.psu.edu/about/university-libraries-strategic-plan/values

Thompson, G.C., Maringanti, H., Anderson, R., Soehner, C.B., & Comer, A. (2019). *Strategic planning for academic libraries: A step-by-step guide.* ALA Editions.

University of Washington. (2016). *Succession Planning Toolkit.* https://hr.uw.edu/pod/wp-content/uploads/sites/10/2018/08/Succession-Planning-Toolkit.pdf

Vaillancourt, A.M. (2022, May 9). How to heal a wounded workgroup you inherit. *The Chronicle of Higher Education.* https://www.chronicle.com/article/how-to-heal-a-wounded-workgroup-you-inherit

Waltz, R.M. (2021). In support of flourishing: Practices to engage, motivate, affirm, and appreciate. *International Information & Library Review, 53*(4), 333–340. 10.1080/10572317. 2021.1990564

Whitaker, M. (2020, July 27). How to be a trauma-informed department chair amid COVID-19. *The Chronicle of Higher Education.* https://www.chronicle.com/article/how-to-be-a-trauma-informed-department-chair-amid-covid-19

Wissinger, C.L., Raish, V., Miller, R.K., & Borrelli, S. (2018). Expert teams in the academic library: Going beyond subject expertise to create scaffolded instruction. *Journal of Library Administration, 58*(4), 313–333. 10.1080/01930826.2018.1448648

4

FROM INDIVIDUAL TO COMMUNITY: BUILDING A COMMUNITY OF PRACTICE AROUND TEACHING

Rachel W. Gammons, Yelena Luckert, Anastasia Armendariz, and Lindsay Inge Carpenter

Introduction

In 2020, the Association of College & Research Libraries (ACRL) granted the University of Maryland (UMD) Libraries their Excellence in Academic Libraries Award in the University Category. Cheryl Middleton, chair of the 2020 Excellence in Academic Libraries Committee, described UMD Libraries as, "stand[ing] out amongst their peers for the development of a robust library staff culture of innovation, as well as their extensive collaborations and engagement with the university's core curriculum, students, and faculty" (Groves, 2020). Although the UMD Libraries is now celebrated for its innovative approach to teaching, this culture of collaboration has not always existed. We offer the UMD Libraries' teaching program as an example of how transformational change around teaching at an academic library can be achieved. Although many of the circumstances are specific to the UMD Libraries, the challenge of reinvigorating an aging and divisive teaching program is not unique to our institution. Our hope is that in reading our experiences, readers will see a reflection of their own libraries and teaching programs and, perhaps, be able to recognize how the foundation for change at their own institutions may already have been laid.

Through this chapter, we explore the transformation of UMD Libraries' teaching efforts from an individualistic approach into a strong community of practice (COP) around teaching based on the mutual affirmation, support, and respect of library teachers. We begin with a history of the UMD Libraries' teaching program, paying special attention to how the program has been shaped by the Libraries' partnership with the UMD Academic Writing Program (ENGL101). Following, we offer an overview of the theoretical framework of Communities of Practice and explore how these concepts have shaped development of COPs at the UMD Libraries using two teacher training initiatives as example: (1) the Research and Teaching Fellowship,

DOI: 10.4324/9781003038634-7

and (2) the Fearless Teaching Institute. We close with a brief consideration of the specific components that have contributed to the transformation of the UMD Libraries' teaching program and offer recommendations for practice.

University of Maryland Libraries Teaching Program

The University of Maryland is the flagship research university for the state of Maryland and supports 31,000 undergraduate students; 10,000 graduate students; and 14,000 faculty and staff across 250 individual academic programs. UMD is a member of the Big Ten Academic Alliance and the University System of Maryland and Affiliated Institutions. The UMD Libraries (the Libraries) are a multi-branch system which employs 59 library faculty members, 99 non-exempt and exempt staff members, 20 colleagues on contract, 13 graduate assistants, and 108 hourly student assistants. Central to the mission of the Libraries is the information literacy teaching program, which serves between 16,000 and 22,000 students per academic year. This instruction is multi-pronged and includes subject specialist librarians, who lead discipline specific information literacy sessions for upper-level undergraduate and graduate students; the Research Education program, which supports graduate students and faculty across the research life cycle; and Teaching and Learning Services (TLS), which manages first-year and general education instruction and provides professional development for library staff around teaching. In recent years, the Libraries has expanded instructional programming to support students through co-curricular workshop series, orientations, and synchronous and asynchronous online courses.

Academic Writing Program

Since 1980, the UMD undergraduate composition program has included a lower-division course, Academic Writing (ENGL101), and an upper-division course, Professional Writing (ENGL39X) (Coogan et al., 2018). These courses work in concert with the UMD Writing Center, which provides co-curricular writing support for undergraduate students. Over the past 30 years, the UMD Libraries has maintained a productive partnership with all elements of the composition program, and in particular, the Academic Writing Program (AWP).

AWP consists of several components with a major emphasis on delivering English 101, a mandatory first-year composition course that develops students' writing and research skills. Each year, around 5,000 first-year students are enrolled in hundreds of ENGL101 sections, taught by dozens of individual instructors, most of whom are adjuncts. Although the UMD general education curricula has changed over the years, Academic Writing (ENGL101) has remained a consistent requirement with few options for testing out of the course (Coogan et al., 2018). As a result, it is one of the few curricular experiences on campus shared by a majority of first year students.

Early on, the Libraries recognized that AWP presented an opportunity to teach foundational information literacy skills to students at the outset of their university career, setting them up for success in their subsequent coursework. Through anecdotal information gleaned from librarians employed during this time, the Libraries' began formalizing information literacy instruction for AWP sections in the late 1980s. In these early days, in-classroom instruction for the program was provided by the reference department of the UMD Undergraduate Library (this branch folded into the main library, McKeldin, in January 2001). During this period, the Libraries' instruction was demand-driven, and the reference librarians taught sporadic one-time sessions within the program (Merikangas, 1999). The requests for in-class instruction came directly from instructors who saw value in having a librarian teach information literacy to their classes. To supplement in-person instruction, the in-house library brochures of that time show that undergraduate librarians also provided one-on-one assistance and conducted scheduled summer orientations to all AWP instructors who desired librarians' help in improving information literacy instruction in their classes. However, while the program showed potential, the small number of Undergraduate Library staff, lack of a dedicated teaching unit in the Libraries, and the large number of AWP sections, kept the Libraries' program from growing beyond its ad-hoc approach.

User Education Services Department

The Libraries went through major organizational changes around 1996–1998 (Baughman, 2008). The areas of subject and general librarianship, including collection development, reference, and instruction, were particularly affected due to full reorganization and merging responsibilities of reference librarians and bibliographers, creating new cadres of subject librarians who combined elements of both subject and generalist work (Lowry, 2005). Along those lines, a new department was formed, User Education Services (UES), with a mission to coordinate and advance the overall University Libraries' information literacy program, as well as assume responsibility for several Undergraduate Library instructional programs, including AWP (Lowry, 2003).

UES took a systematic approach to teaching information literacy, including solidifying the earlier programmatic attempts with AWP. In the mid-1990s, AWP was going through its own administrative and curricular changes, and UES became more motivated to work directly with the AWP administration, rather than individual instructors. Shortly after, information literacy instruction was formally incorporated in the ENGL101 syllabus, which dramatically increased the requests for instruction sessions. The "University of Maryland Libraries Instruction Statistics Report: 1997," which was compiled by UES on behalf of all library staff who teach information literacy skills, provides a glimpse of the program and its new direction. According to this report, in the 1996–1997 academic year, UES taught 141 AWP classes, which were attended by 2,911 students. This program was (and continues to be) an enormous undertaking; particularly for one led by a single department.

Academic Writing Program and Teaching Assistants

One of the initial barriers for the Libraries in growing the information literacy program for AWP was a lack of participation from librarians. Most staff librarians strongly opposed participation due to work overload in other areas, including newly assigned subject responsibilities and other instructional and reference obligations. Around the same time, University of Maryland librarians became faculty, and the newly minted faculty librarians grappled with increased expectations for service and scholarship requirements. Without sufficient librarians to do this work, and to avoid possible staff conflicts, UES resorted to hiring temporary instructors, known as Teaching Assistants (TAs) to teach library instruction for all AWP courses. TAs came from many academic programs but were primarily composed of graduate students from the University of Maryland College of Library and Information Services (presently, College of Information Studies or iSchool). TAs were hourly employees contracted on a semester-basis and typically taught one or more information literacy sessions per academic term.

By 2013, UES had solidified and consolidated the instructional approach for AWP, including renaming the instructional sessions "Library Day" and developing a new curriculum based around developing search strategies and navigating library resources. During the 2013-14 academic year about 200 AWP sections were taught by the Libraries, representing a 40% increase from the decade prior. Most, if not all, of the teaching was done by TAs hired by UES for this specific purpose. However, in comparison with previous years, far fewer TAs were hired despite the increased load of AWP classes. While there were 39 TAs hired in 1997, in 2013, UES hired only 6. Each TA was compensated at $15/per hour and expected to teach between 20 and 30 sessions over a six-week period of the semester, estimated to be from mid-September to the end of October, and mid-February to the end of March. This would have been a substantial teaching load for a seasoned librarian but was particularly problematic given the majority of the TAs were minimally trained graduate students in their first semester of teaching.

The turnover among TAs was high. Often, these students were hired with no prior experience working in the library setting, teaching experience, or familiarity with campus. Yet, this was an attractive job to many iSchool students. It paid better than most library hourly positions on campus, required relatively limited time commitment, and offered invaluable experience for future librarians. Unfortunately, due to the Libraries' budget timetable, these students were often hired in August, just before the fall semester began, which did not offer sufficient time to properly train and prepare TAs to deliver information literacy instruction to thousands of first year students. To compensate, UES developed a "Library Day Training Manual: A Guide for Lecturers" for newly hired instructors. It described the AWP program, covered expectations of library adjuncts, provided lesson plans, and included some information about the Libraries. In addition, each library instructor (which included both TAs and a small number of subject librarians who continued to teach AWP sessions) were provided with a teaching script and slide deck that included screenshots of the Libraries website. Improvisation or adjustments to these materials were discouraged. Although these efforts were better than none, they were not nearly enough to properly prepare and develop library instructors. As a result, the program continued to present difficulties for both instructors and the Libraries.

A Program Divided

Like many academic libraries, UMD Libraries fell into the trap of isolating the administrative work of teaching within a single unit or position. As Arellano Douglas and Gadsby (2019) note, instructional coordinator positions emerge when an instructional program grows to or beyond a point that it requires coordination. Although the instruction coordinator or unit may reduce administrative overhead, it can also silo administrative responsibility and functional support for teaching with a single person or unit. By 2013, the Libraries' instructional programming had reached this point. On one side, UES operated an efficient and tightly managed instructional program, driven primarily by AWP instruction, which relied heavily on hourly student labor, detailed lesson plans, centralized scheduling, and standardized outcomes-based assessment. On the other side, subject librarians led an expansive but largely self-directed teaching program for upper-level undergraduate and graduate students. Although each could have benefited from the skills and experiences of the other, there was little collaboration across departments (Carroll et al., 2014).

Teaching and Learning Services

In late 2013, UES was rebranded Teaching and Learning Services (TLS) and joined a newly formed department focused on undergraduate learning. Although this strengthened the TLS portfolio, it also exacerbated the organizational division between instructional and subject librarians, which was already showing signs of strain. In 2014, a series of staff vacancies offered an opportunity to again rethink the organizational structure, and in October 2014, TLS was moved to its current home in the Research, Teaching, and Learning Department. This offered two benefits. First, it situated the head of TLS in the same reporting chain as the subject liaison librarians. Second, it consolidated the Libraries' teaching efforts within a single department. Although this organizational shift may seem insignificant, the realignment of TLS was the catalyst to transforming the Libraries' teaching program. Today, the TLS unit sits at the heart of a vibrant information literacy teaching program that invites creativity and collaboration from across the Libraries (Gammons & Inge, 2017).

Moving Forward

We share our story with the understanding that while our organizational structure may be unique, our experience is not. Like many academic libraries, the increase in information literacy instruction in the late 1990s and early 2000s led the UMD Libraries to quickly develop instructional librarian positions, which became institutionalized within the organizational culture. As was typical for large academic libraries of the time, these duties were substantial enough to require the establishment of a dedicated instructional unit. Over the years, as true for many academic libraries, teaching became a specialized skill that was segregated from the day-to-day work of the Libraries. As a result, the teaching program became divisive, pitting instruction librarians against subject librarians, and new teachers against experienced instructors. However, over the past five years, the UMD Libraries teaching program has transformed into a strong and unified COP that uplifts, affirms, supports, challenges, and improves teaching at every level. Our hope is that in sharing our process of transformational change, we inspire others to see the potential for growth in their teaching programs and identify pathways to overcome the obstacles they may face.

A New Community of Practice

A community of practice is a group of individuals who encourage one another to improve their knowledge or practice through mutual support, shared labor, and intellectual pursuit (Wenger, 1998). Over the past seven years, the UMD Libraries has developed a strong COP around teaching and learning. Participants in the program include a variety of staff members ranging from tenured faculty librarians, to first year graduate students, to early career professionals. Although there have been many changes that have helped to shift the culture toward collaboration, we focus on two areas in which we have intentionally cultivated a COP: the Research and Teaching Fellowship, a teacher training program for MLIS students, and The Fearless Teaching Program, an in-house professional development program for library teachers. Each leveraged existing resources by using an established partnership or program as foundation, started small with the implementation of a pilot program, and involved collaboration from across the Libraries. Our intent is to focus not on the day-to-day logistics of programmatic organization and management, which has been covered extensively in other articles, but, instead, to highlight *why* the programs have been successful in fostering COPs and how these principles could be employed at other Libraries.

Literature Review

"Communities of practice are groups of people who share a concern or passion for something they do and learn how to do it better as they interact regularly" (Wenger, 2011, p. 1). A term coined by Jean Lave and Etienne Wenger in 1991, communities of practice facilitate the exchange of knowledge and technical skills through three interpersonal practices: mutual engagement, joint enterprise, and shared repertoire (Wenger, 1998). These components blend process and product and lead to the creation of communal resources, which might include toolkits, programming, stories, or even motivating concepts.

In 2015, Wenger shared three further characteristics of a COP: domain, community, and practice (p. 2). The domain refers to a shared commitment and competence, which is pursued collectively by the community. Through information sharing activities and discussions, members learn from one another. They also facilitate the formation of trusting relationships. Members with varied experiences and backgrounds feel more welcomed in, and significant to, the community. Building on the shared repertoire, the final characteristic of practice distinguishes this community from an affinity group. After the initial production of resources, activities, and models that were created from shared ideas and perspectives, sustained conversations, reflection, and projects between members are intended to refine the practice itself.

Communities of Practice in Higher Education

COPs often focus on apprenticeship in the context of a range of vocations. Whether midwifery or tailoring, learning—particularly situated learning, where increased participation transformed newcomers into experienced practitioners—is paramount (Lave & Wenger, 1991, p. 72). With learning comes teaching. Educators across contexts have implemented COPs. Through case studies and reviews over the past three decades, there is consensus that a COP can both center and improve teaching and learning objectives. As principles of COP have taken shape as ongoing professional development circles (Laksov et al., 2008; Patton & Parker, 2017; Vescio et al., 2008), COPs have also incubated broader shifts in teaching, including student-centered learning (Vescio et al., 2008).

In higher education, COPs have been implemented in a range of instructional contexts (Patton & Parker, 2017). Most case studies have focused on qualitative data, with documentation of the support of teachers for various COPs. More rigorous overviews of methodology and quantitative metrics beyond test scores, and even qualitative results from learners other than teachers will reflect a fuller realization of Wenger's hope for COPs in teaching that transforms teaching in three spheres: internally around subject matter, externally "beyond the walls of the school," and over the longer lifetime of students (2011, p. 5; Vescio et al., 2008).

Communities of Practice in Libraries

Speaking to the teaching and learning components of contemporary librarianship as well as the practicability of COP across vocations, the adoption of COP by libraries is considered a key strategy to advance the mission and impact of a library (Kim, 2015, p. 49). The iterative nature of a COP is particularly valuable in a library. Patron needs unfold across a shifting landscape of institutional priorities and technologies, making communities of other practitioners with similar priorities and goals essential in refining one's ability to meet and even exceed those needs (Green, 2014; Osborn, 2017; Smith & Lee, 2016).

A mutually beneficial COP can develop within a single library (Osborn, 2017); they can also form virtually and take the shape of forums that connect—and advance—the work of librarians working in shared domains (Louque, 2021). Within the context of an academic library, Gannon-Leary and Fontainha's (2007) foundational work on virtual learning in a COP presents a call for awareness of the legal issues and potential for an erosion of the trusting, close relationships that ought to characterize a COP in cross-institutional and virtual COPs worth returning to in these emerging contexts.

Benefits of COP in Libraries

Just as a COP in teaching accelerates, and not simply reacts to, advances in pedagogy, so can a COP within libraries (Green 2014; Kim, 2015; Smith & Lee, 2016). When these advances add to the already extensive duties of librarians, COPs can provide spaces of commiseration as much as vocation-related resources (Smith & Lee, 2016, p. 120). Dedication of a COP to ongoing knowledge transfer and the creation of usable resources will also reduce the knowledge loss when members of the COP leave it (Louque, 2021, p. 63).

Much of the literature on COPs in libraries considers the continuing professional development of practitioners (Louque, 2021; Osborn, 2017; Smith & Lee, 2016, p. 68). Kim's (2015) article guides us back to Wenger's view of a COP as an apprenticeship that extends the potential of COPs to emerging professionals as both learners and key contributors. A COP "is an effective way of learning that helps students internalize the knowledge that they obtain from classroom activities through practice" (Kim, 2015, p. 49). A COP that is inclusive of emerging library professionals will not only integrate their perspectives and experiences to the benefit of the library at large, it can bridge the "considerable gap between the needs of academic libraries and the training MLIS students receive" (Gammons et al., 2018, p. 334). Supportive COPs were also cited as key combatants of imposter syndrome endemic to new academic and instructional librarians (Martinez & Forrey, 2019).

Example 1: Research and Teaching Fellowship

By 2015, the UMD Libraries were ready for change. The organizational restructuring of UES to TLS; realignment of the TLS unit into the Research, Teaching, and Learning Department; and staffing changes at the unit and department levels offered an opportunity to reexamine the TLS portfolio. At the time, the unit supported information literacy instruction for several legacy courses that had been developed by UES. Although the AWP was by far the most demanding, other courses, such as First Year Experience (UNIV100) had grown to a point that they also required dozens of information literacy sessions. Almost all of these sessions were led by hourly student workers, or TAs.

Over the years, the TA position had become an institutional crutch. The influx of temporary labor enabled the Libraries to grow programs that would otherwise have been limited by staffing levels, but by the same token, the high turnover, limited training and support, and administrative maintenance set a low ceiling for the type and quality of teaching that could be supported by these positions. To maintain a standard of quality around teaching, UES embraced increasingly authoritarian measures, including ever more detailed teaching scripts, slide decks, and intensive teaching schedules. By 2013, the TA positions had become problematic for all parties. The students in the positions were not well-supported; UES administrators were struggling to maintain the logistical and administrative responsibilities; and the academic programs served by the TAs were becoming increasingly frustrated with the quality of instruction they received.

In 2015, the new head of TLS partnered with subject librarians and other colleagues to redesign the Libraries' approach to first year instruction. A strengths, weaknesses, opportunities, and threats (SWOT) analysis of the unit revealed several redundancies in programming. For example, many of the students who attended information literacy sessions for AWP were also attending sessions for first year experience. Because the TLS teaching calendar was so compressed, these sessions often occurred within weeks or days of one another. On top of this, much of the content was duplicated between the various courses. In their post-session assessments, students reported feeling bored, confused, and disinterested in the content of the sessions. The SWOT analysis showed clearly that the TLS unit was doing too many things, and none of them well. In short, the teaching program had grown beyond the capacity of the unit. Rather than recognizing and honoring those limitations, the former UES/TLS administrators had attempted to subvert constraints by leaning more heavily into standardization and control. Any attempt to change the culture around teaching had to start here, dismantling the toxic approach to teaching that formed the foundation of the Libraries' teaching program.

The first step in this process was to scale back involvement with low-demand courses, such as first year experience. Although these courses required less oversight than AWP, they diverted time, attention, and resources away from the anchor program, which was (and remains still) AWP. Wherever possible, in-person sessions for "splinter courses," such as first year experience, were replaced by asynchronous self-paced online tutorials that could be incorporated into the course by interested instructors. This allowed students who might have already received library instruction to advance through content that might have been repeated in earlier sessions, while enabling students who had not been exposed to library resources to receive the detailed information literacy instruction that would help them to succeed in their assignments.

The second step was to change the timing, preparation, and hiring process for the Libraries' TA program. One of the challenges of the TA position had been the high turnover and limited window for training. By consolidating the TLS instructional programming and reducing the number of courses being served, we were able to redirect the financial resources back into the TA program. From this emerged the Research and Teaching Fellowship (RTF); a three-semester teacher training and professional development program for Masters of Library and Information Science (MLIS) students.

A New Model for Student Teachers

Rather than hiring part-time instructors in August, as had been the previous practice, fellows begin the RTF program in the spring semester, when the number of library instruction sessions is less demanding. While TAs were contracted from semester to semester (often failing to return after a single semester), fellows commit to the RTF program for a full three semesters, beginning with their second semester in the MLIS program and concluding with their fourth and final semester. In May 2015, the Libraries hired the first cohort of fellows, compressing the first semester of reading, discussion, co-teaching, and observation into a 10-week summer pilot program. Since then, RTF has grown into a dynamic community of teachers that gives back to the Libraries and the professional and campus communities. In exchange for their participation, fellows receive invaluable teaching experience, professional development support, and a supportive peer cohort. By investing in the fellows, the Libraries is able to offer high-quality information literacy instruction to thousands of AWP students per year and also able to give back to the profession by training future academic librarians. Although it is not the focus of this chapter, we would be remiss not to mention that RTF is a cost-effective program, with a total annual cost of less than half that of a single graduate assistantship position. To date, RTF has a 100% professional job placement rate, including more than 25 alumni at academic and research institutions across the country.

Earlier works have documented in depth the operation, administration, and assessment of the RTF program (Gammons & Inge, 2017; Gammons et al., 2018; Gammons et al., in press). Rather than duplicate these efforts, we focus here on the elements of the RTF program that have helped to develop a COP and, in particular, those components which have helped to shift the broader culture around teaching at UMD Libraries. As noted earlier, COPs share three characteristics: the existence of a shared enterprise or domain; mutual engagement and community; and shared repertoire or practice (Wenger, 2015). We offer our examination using this framework as a guide.

Shared Enterprise

In the context of the RTF program, the "shared enterprise" is the mission to provide high-quality information literacy instruction to undergraduate students enrolled in AWP. That mission is achieved through structured opportunities for mutual engagement and shared practice. For example, fellows commit to enrolling in a 1-credit course each semester of their 3-semester fellowship. This 1-credit course meets weekly, and provides an opportunity to review standardized teaching materials, analyze pedagogical theory, and discuss strategies for in-person and virtual instruction. Although the curriculum for these courses is set by RTF directors, fellows are encouraged to bring questions and agenda items as they arise, particularly during weeks with heavy instructional loads. This allows fellows and TLS librarians to collaboratively address teaching challenges in real time, sharing tools and techniques to improve teacher confidence as well as student experience. Throughout the RTF program, there is an emphasis on reflection and growth. During their first semester of independent teaching, TLS staff conduct multiple teaching observations for each fellow. During their second semester of teaching, fellows scaffold these skills to conduct mutual peer teaching observations for one another. These observations are structured as opportunities to celebrate growth and strategize areas for improvement, rather than as punitive surveillance practices (Alabi & Weare, 2014). Observations are bookended by (1) pre-observation surveys where fellows can indicate areas where they would (or would not) like feedback, and (2) post-observation consultations to debrief about the session and address any of the fellows' concerns. In addition to completing observation worksheets with their peers, fellows also engage in reflective journaling to process what they gain from observing colleagues.

Mutual Engagement and Community

In addition to class sessions, fellows engage in community through shared office hours. For one hour each week, individual fellows hold office hours that overlap with at least one other cohort member. Fellows can use this time to communicate with AWP instructors, conduct reference consultations, prepare for instruction, or discuss teaching challenges and successes with their peers and/or TLS staff. Initial iterations of RTF did not require fellows to ensure that their office hours overlapped with at least one other person's; however, based on graduating fellows' feedback that these informal opportunities for community were essential to improving their practice and sense of belonging (Gammons et al., 2018), RTF directors now prioritize shared office hours as a key component of the RTF COP.

RTF also fosters community beyond the fellowship by hosting a monthly journal club discussion around a recently published article related to library instruction, which is open to any library staff member or MLIS student (Gammons et al., 2018). In 2020, TLS staff also launched the RTF Alumni Network to better connect current and former fellows. The RTF Alumni Network includes regular communications, such as a bi-annual newsletter highlighting professional achievements of current and former fellows, and a listserv to share job advertisements, research and professional opportunities, and to get support from members of the community (Gammons et al., in press). The sense of community and mutual engagement was, and remains still, the heart of the RTF program.

Shared Repertoire

In contrast to the authoritarian approach employed by UES, RTF relies upon a shared repertoire that is collaboratively developed, assessed, and refined by the contributions of each cohort of fellows. Using the standard ENGL101 syllabus as a guide, TLS staff develop adaptable information literacy lesson plans that support specific assignments and meet the Libraries' learning outcomes. Fellows are invited to provide feedback on the lesson plans and adapt materials in consultation with their AWP faculty partner, based on student needs and their own teaching style. To support new fellows and streamline the sometimes-cumbersome scheduling process, TLS staff provide shared email communication templates and faculty questionnaires to guide negotiations about the type of content and support provided in an information literacy session. These templates help build fellows' confidence when directly communicating with AWP faculty. They also help to define a consistent communication style between the Libraries and AWP. As with all materials, the communication templates are fully customizable and intended to serve as launching points, rather than directives.

In 2020, with the shift to virtual instruction because of the COVID-19 pandemic, TLS staff recognized the need to provide even greater support for fellows who were adapting to independent teaching in a new modality. In response, TLS staff developed slide decks to complement the lesson plans (Gammons et al., in press). As with the lesson plans, fellows were free to adapt the slide decks to suit their needs, or to forego use entirely. Fellows often chose to share their adaptations with their cohort, leading to improvements in the standardized slide decks and further opportunities for discussion about virtual teaching strategies.

Creating a Community That Lasts

Through these and other strategies, RTF builds trust between fellows and librarians, which, in turn, improves the quality of the Libraries' teaching program. Each year, we conduct a focus group with graduating fellows to identify opportunities for improvement in the RTF program. The feedback we hear most often is that fellows crave a sense of community. In fact, fellows cite this as the most important benefit of RTF; even more so than opportunities for mentorship, job application support, or professional experience (Gammons et al., 2018). Through the operation of the RTF program, we have learned that a sense of community is earned, not given. Creating a COP has required that we not only develop strong teaching tools and administrative procedures, but also that we make repeated and intentional investments in building the interpersonal relationships between teachers. Today, RTF is a strong COP that includes current fellows, library staff members, and alumni. Although we are proud to have created such a program, we know that the continuation and sustenance of the RTF community is dependent on our willingness to prioritize relationships, as well as teaching.

Example 2: Fearless Teaching Institute

By 2017, the TLS unit had hired additional staff, reached a full faculty complement, and relationships between TLS and subject librarians had improved. The Libraries had also developed a close working relationship with the UMD Teaching and Learning Transformation Center (TLTC), which was, at the time, offering a self-paced professional development program for faculty called the Launch Certificate. The Launch Certificate required that participants complete a set number of experiences, including teaching workshops, faculty learning communities, and classroom teaching observations. Although there were several librarians who expressed interest in completing the Launch Certificate, most of the activities were oriented toward traditional teaching faculty, and it was difficult for librarians to complete the necessary requirements.

One of the core components of RTF is a "Teaching as Research" project, a semester-long partnership between a senior fellow and subject librarian in which they work together to design (or redesign) an upper-level undergraduate or graduate-level information literacy class (Gammons et al., 2018). Throughout the RTF program, Fellows are introduced to pedagogical concepts ranging from backwards design, to learning outcomes assessment, to successful mentorship practices. The Teaching as Research projects not only strengthened relationships between subject librarians, the TLS unit, and the RTF program, but have also provided opportunities for librarians to learn techniques from the fellows, and for fellows to benefit from the experiences and expertise of the librarians. Although the success of the Teaching as Research projects suggested that librarians might benefit from more formalized opportunities to engage with new approaches to pedagogy and practice, until recently, it had been difficult to find ways to scale the content from the RTF to the broader Libraries staff.

Around this same time, TLTC was piloting the Fearless Teaching Framework, a research-based conceptual mapping of the foundational processes that contribute to effective teaching, including:

- classroom climate,
- course content,
- teaching practice, and
- assessment strategies (Donlan et al., 2019).

Using the Fearless Teaching Framework and Launch Certificate as inspiration, TLS staff developed a pilot program called the UMD Libraries' Fearless Teaching Institute (FTI). The Institute would offer the benefits of the TLTC programming in a format targeted to library instructors. Originally designed as a self-paced certificate program, the FTI pilot program offered opportunities for librarians to improve their teaching climate, content, practice, and assessment through in-house teaching workshops, peer teaching observations, and journal club discussions.

Since its launch in 2018, FTI has become an agile arm of the UMD Libraries teaching program with a mission to deepen and strengthen library instruction at all levels, from staff training to advanced information literacy instruction. Although it began as a certificate program, FTI has evolved beyond its humble beginnings to include a variety of programming, including teaching workshops, informal and formal discussions, peer teaching observations, and office hours. FTI programs are offered both online and in-person; however online has become the predominant mode to maximize participation (Gammons et al., in press).

Shared Enterprise

The joint enterprise of the FTI COP is accomplished through the shared goals of

- improving individual teaching skill, competence, and confidence, and
- strengthening the Libraries' overall instruction program.

During the 2020–2021 academic year, the FTI hosted more than 50 events with a combined attendance of more than 400 library faculty, staff, and student workers (Gammons et al., in press). Participants in the FTI have a variety of pedagogical needs, including improving training programs for newly hired student workers, strengthening advanced research strategies for faculty, and leading data services workshops. As a result, the FTI focuses on pedagogical theories, teaching techniques, and learning tools that are broadly applicable, rather than targeting a specific discipline, course, or program. Across all FTI programming, there is a shared and consistent goal of supporting library teachers and improving learning opportunities for the UMD campus community.

Mutual Engagement & Community

As was the case for RTF, the FTI COP began with formalized opportunities for mutual engagement, such as peer teaching observations, and has expanded to include an informal community that offers support to one another outside of FTI events. Although the FTI includes a variety of programmatic offerings, at the heart of the FTI program are structured teaching workshops. Importantly, the topics, format, and goals of the workshops are developed collaboratively. Although TLS staff provide administrative leadership by scheduling, advertising, and leading most of the FTI workshops, library staff are encouraged to submit topics for future workshops or offer their expertise as workshop leaders. Over the last year, library staff have contributed their ideas and facilitation skills for a variety of workshops. For example, in the 2020–2021 academic year, the Coordinator for Reference Services suggested an FTI series on approaching reference as a form of teaching. Over the spring 2020 semester, subject liaison librarians took turns leading workshops on essential resources and common questions in their subject areas.

These workshops were open to anyone in the Libraries and were particularly well attended by RTF Fellows and graduate assistants.

An important philosophy underlying the FTI is valuing the expertise and experience of its participants, whether they are new professionals or tenured librarians with years of experience. This synthesis of diverse experiences and perspectives is seen in monthly journal club discussions. A joint venture between the RTF and the FTI, journal clubs are co-facilitated by fellows, with participation from throughout the Libraries (Gammons et al., 2018). Not only do these discussions offer opportunities to stay current with literature on academic librarianship, but they also build community among Libraries staff members who might not otherwise have opportunities for collaboration. Through these discussions, fellows, graduate assistants, and other student workers are given an equal seat at the table with established librarians, experienced staff members, and administrators. The participants learn from one another's experiences and analysis of the selected readings for that session.

Through their participation in the FTI workshops and journal clubs, participants form relationships with colleagues who might work outside of their functional areas but share similar research interests and/or professional goals. As a result, collaboration continues outside the formal programming, with FTI participants consulting each other on lesson plans, online learning tools, and assessment instruments. Rather than viewing teaching as an isolated or individual experience, participants have come to view their colleagues as a ready source of support and have embraced instructional collaboration as a way to strengthen practice, rather than an admission of weakness.

Shared Repertoire

To document the expertise shared in the FTI programs, the TLS unit manages an FTI research guide, which serves the dual purpose of repository for FTI materials and advertising upcoming programs. In the spirit of the COP, the production of these materials works to strengthen the sense of community, which enhances the product (teaching), which is, in turn, redirected back into the COP through the continual refinement of the FTI program. One of the most successful examples of shared repertoire in the FTI COP is the development of the peer teaching observation program.

Although peer teaching observations are an important component of the RTF COP, at the time of the FTI pilot, the practice was not common in the Libraries. Taking inspiration from the TLTC Launch Certificate—which included a formal teaching observation as one of its requirements—the FTI pilot program asked participants to complete at least one reciprocal teaching observation with a colleague. While there was interest from library staff around peer observation, many librarians were apprehensive about inviting anyone, even a trusted colleague, into their classroom to offer critique. To reduce anxiety, TLS librarians worked with subject librarians to develop a formal peer observation program plan, which included a list of best-practices, procedures, and templates that could be used to guide peer observations and post-observation discussions (Gammons, 2018). As a soft launch to the program, TLS staff hosted an FTI workshop on peer observations. During the workshop, a TLS librarian "observed" the workshop, and the session concluded with a mock debrief between the observer and the workshop facilitator. Like the RTF, in which the communication templates and teaching materials had supported the transition to online teaching for the fellows, the peer teaching observation templates, program tools, and workshop helped to ease participants into the new environment of peer observation and foster trust between participants. In addition to the formal FTI peer-observation program—which is offered by the FTI every third year - informal teaching observations are now a part of the culture at UMD Libraries.

Creating a Community that Lasts

As with the RTF, the FTI has required a balance between offering the administrative support necessary for a large and complex instructional program to succeed, while encouraging the creativity and innovation that makes the content and experience appealing to participants. Although the TLS unit offers logistical and programmatic support for the FTI, the success of the program emerges from the sense of shared responsibility that extends beyond the unit. Library staff routinely send TLS staff ideas for new workshops, offer suggestions for speakers, and forward relevant readings or professional development opportunities that might inspire new programming. The feeling of shared ownership of the FTI, or as Wenger (2011) would describe it, *mutual engagement*, generates enthusiasm for the FTI programming. As a result, events are well attended. To put it simply, the FTI program belongs to no one, and because of that, it belongs to everyone. It is the sense of community and shared responsibility that have made the FTI COP successful.

Conclusion

Today, the UMD Libraries teaching program is almost unrecognizable from the program that existed a decade prior. Changes in staffing, programming, and a renewed sense of enthusiasm and purpose have encouraged the development of new teaching programs and processes. In addition, the intentional cultivation of COPs has led to a strong comradery among staff, which has in turn strengthened the Libraries' teaching. Although many of the challenges presented were specific to our institution, our hope is that through this discussion, readers have seen a reflection of their own libraries and teaching programs. In conclusion, we offer two recommendations for librarians who may be interested in pursuing transformational change around teaching, which can be applied regardless of institutional size or type.

Support from Library Administrators

One of the biggest contributors to the success of our teaching program has been visible support from library administration. Library leaders at every level, from unit heads to senior administrators, routinely attend FTI and RTF events, such as journal club discussions or teaching workshops. Administrators have also offered tangible expressions of support. For example, to support the launch of the FTI pilot program, the director for the Research, Teaching, and Learning (RTL) department offered one hour of the department's monthly two-hour-long meeting to dedicate to a teaching workshop; which ensured that everyone in the RTL department would be able to attend. This early participation laid the groundwork for the program and helped to build enthusiasm for the FTI program. During annual reviews for librarians, administrators praised librarians' participation in FTI events or support of the RTF program. While these gestures may seem small, the transformation of our teaching program would not have been possible without their support.

In our experience, while administrators are happy to offer their support, they are best positioned to succeed when we are able to articulate the ways that they can be helpful to us. For example, early in the RTF program, the head of TLS sent individualized invitations to library administrators inviting them to journal club, which specified how their presence would benefit the discussion. Other examples have included requests for financial support to offer coffee and pastries for early morning events, inviting administrators to program planning meetings to communicate the often-invisible labor of instructional oversight and endorsements for specific events or opportunities. Our experience shows that while administrative support conveys importance, importance leads to participation, and participation leads to community. All of this begins with advocating for why and how a teaching program matters.

Intentional Cultivation of Community

Through the RTF and the FTI, we learned that, although participants often desire community, they need support in building the relationships that enable a community to flourish. This type of support can include formal experiences, such as offering teaching workshops, but can also focus on providing the administrative or logistical support for informal opportunities for mutual engagement, such as a peer teaching observation program, journal club discussions, or overlapping office hours. Our experience in developing COPs at UMD Libraries leads us to believe that while a sense of community cannot be manufactured or forced, it can be encouraged. Often, as instruction coordinators, we focus on the big programs, new tools, and exciting trends. But in building community, it is often paying attention to small, multi-faceted, and seemingly insignificant ways that we build relationships that can lead to a sincere and lasting COP.

References

Alabi, J., & Weare, Jr., W.H. (2014). Peer review of teaching: Best practices for a non-programmatic approach. *Communications in Information Literacy*, 8(2), 180–191. 10.15760/comminfolit.2014.8.2.171

Arellano Douglas, V., & Gadsby, J. (2019). All carrots, no sticks: Relational practice and library instruction coordination. *In the Library with the Lead Pipe*. http://www.inthelibrarywiththeleadpipe.org/2019/all-carrots-no-sticks-relational-practice-and-library-instruction-coordination/

Baughman, M.S. (2008). Assessment of teams and teamwork in the University of Maryland Libraries. *portal: Libraries and the Academy*, 8(3), 293–312. 10.1353/pla.0.0005

Carroll, A., Lindquist, E., Hudson S., & Cleary, L. (2014). *General instruction task force report*. University of Maryland Libraries. 10.13016/M2HB3W

Coogan, R., Donawerth, J., & Scanlon, M. (2018). Innovation and restoration: A history of introductory academic writing at the University of Maryland. In S.W. Logan & W. Slater, W. (Eds.), *Academic and professional writing in an age of accountability* (pp. 13–23). Southern Illinois University Press.

Donlan, A.E., Loughlin, S.M., & Byrne, V.L. (2019). The Fearless Teaching Framework: A model to synthesize foundational education research for university instructors. *To Improve the Academy*, 38(1), 33–49. 10.1002/tia2.20087

Gammons, R.W., & Inge, L.T. (2017). Using the ACRL framework to develop a student-centered model for program-level assessment. *Communications in Information Literacy*, 11(1), 168–184. 10.15760/comminfolit.2017.11.1.40

Gammons, R.W. (2018). *Peer teaching observation program*. University of Maryland Libraries. http://hdl.handle.net/1903/28051

Gammons, R.W., Carroll, A.J., & Carpenter, L.I. (2018). "I never knew I could be a teacher": A student-centered MLIS fellowship for future teacher-librarians. *Portal: Libraries and the Academy* 18(2), 331–362. 10.1353/pla.2018.0019

Gammons, R.W., Carpenter, L.I., Wilson, S., & Shaw, B. (in press). Keep teaching: Using disruption as a catalyst for change [Special Issue]. *portal: Libraries and the Academy*.

Gannon-Leary, P., & Fontainha, E. (2007). Communities of practice and virtual learning communities: benefits, barriers and success factors. *eLearning Papers*, No. 5, 1–13. https://ssrn.com/abstract=1018066

Green, H.E. (2014). Facilitating communities of practice in digital humanities: librarian collaborations for research and training in text encoding. *The Library Quarterly*, 84 (2), 219–234, 10.1086/675332

Groves, K. (2020, January 4). *University of Maryland wins ACRL Excellence in Academic Libraries Award*. ARL News. https://www.arl.org/news/university-of-maryland-wins-acrl-excellence-in-academic-libraries-award-2020/

Kim, J. (2015) Integrating communities of practice into library services. *Collaborative Librarianship*, 7 (2), 47–55. https://digitalcommons.du.edu/collaborativelibrarianship/vol7/iss2/2/

Laksov, K.B., Mann, S., & Dahlgren, L.O. (2008). Developing a community of practice around teaching: a case study. *Higher Education Research & Development*, 27(2), 121–132. 10.1080/07294360701805259

Lave, J., & Wenger, E. (1991). *Situated learning: Legitimate peripheral participation*. Cambridge University Press.

Louque, J.G. (2021). Exploring the value of communities of practice in academic libraries. *Codex*, 6(1), 54–76. https://journal.acrlla.org/index.php/codex/article/view/188

Lowry, C.B. (2003). *The ubiquitous library: University of Maryland Libraries in the next five years, new directions & continuing legacy.* University of Maryland Libraries. 10.13016/5yuu-hywe

Lowry, C.B. (2005). Continuous organizational development – teamwork, learning leadership, and measurement. *Portal: Libraries and the Academy, 5*(1), 1–6. 10.1353/pla.2005.0010

Martinez, J., & Forrey, M. (2019). Overcoming imposter syndrome: The adventures of two new instruction librarians. *Reference Services Review, 47*(3), 331–342. 10.1108/RSR-03-2 019-0021

Merikangas, R.J. (1999). *Historical and heuristic frameworks for shared governance in academic libraries: A documentary history, interpretation, and questions for the library council and others of the University of Maryland* (ED441516). ERIC. https://eric.ed.gov/?id=ED441516

Osborn, J. (2017). Librarians as teachers: forming a learning and teaching community of practice. *Journal of the Australian Library and Information Association, 66*(2), 162–169. 10.1 080/24750158.2017.1328633

Patton, K., & Parker, M. (2017). Teacher education communities of practice: More than a culture of collaboration. *Teaching and Teacher Education, 67*, 351–360. 10.1016/j.tate.201 7.06.013

Smith, B., & Lee, L. (2016). Librarians and OER: Cultivating a community of practice to be more effective advocates. *Journal of Library & Information Services in Distance Learning, 11*(1-2), 106–122. 10.1080/1533290x.2016.1226592

Vescio, V., Ross, D., & Adams, A. (2008). A review of research on the impact of professional learning communities on teaching practice and student learning. *Teaching and Teacher Education, 24*(1), 80–91. 10.1016/j.tate.2007.01.004

Wenger, E. (2011, October 20). *Communities of practice: A brief introduction.* Scholars' Bank, University of Oregon. http://hdl.handle.net/1794/11736

Wenger, E. (1998). *Communities of practice: Learning, meaning and identity.* Cambridge University Press.

Wenger-Trayner. (2015, April 15). Communities of practice: A brief introduction. https://wenger-trayner.com/wp-content/uploads/2015/04/07-Brief-introduction-to-communities-of-practice.pdf

PART III
Curriculum Development

5

INSTRUCTION BY DESIGN: EMBEDDING THE LIBRARY INTO CURRICULUM DESIGN

Rachel I. Wightman

Introduction

Academic librarians have long worked with faculty on their campuses to varying degrees on curriculum design. These collaborations often focus on a few specific areas of librarianship, including information literacy instruction (ILI) and collection development. It is not unusual for academic librarians to also be assigned liaison or subject areas they work with more closely on these things.

A brief review of the literature shows many examples of librarians collaborating with faculty, often within a specific discipline context. Brasley (2008) outlines various effective collaborations from multiple institutions around the United States, offering a framework for collaborations, including identifying learning outcomes and assessment. Most of these faculty-librarian collaborations occurred within specific disciplines, such as nursing, political science, and biology. Similarly, Farrell and Badke (2015) discuss the importance of situating ILI within a specific discipline to enhance students' understanding of information literacy concepts.

These discipline-specific examples highlight the ways in which librarians have historically engaged with faculty primarily within their liaison areas. These small-scale, subject-specific collaborations are incredibly important to students' understanding of information literacy and research. However, they can also result in a piecemeal approach to ILI as students in different disciplines experience different levels of library instruction, depending on how the instruction or liaison librarian worked with the teaching faculty. Additionally, liaison or instruction librarians who are particularly skilled at outreach or curriculum and research design may become 'victims of their own success'—becoming overwhelmed by requests to collaborate—while other librarians have less to do. This approach can result in uneven or inconsistent ILI across disciplines.

DOI: 10.4324/9781003038634-9

Another challenge with finding ways to embed library services or ILI into the curriculum or with faculty collaborations is the shift many universities are making to online, asynchronous learning. Historically many academic librarians have relied on the 'one-shot' instruction session to provide ILI to students. With asynchronous classes, librarians need to learn or find new ways of providing instruction, such as tutorials, guides, and videos, which do not involve a live session with a librarian. With these kinds of tools, it can be challenging to create instruction programs that are both personal and sustainable in the new higher education environment. Moran and Mulvihill (2017) note the challenges with balancing personalized ILI with sustainable practices in asynchronous classes, while providing ILI to as many students as possible.

As the higher education landscape continues to change, librarians' roles are also shifting. Johnson (2018) references the many areas in which reference and liaison librarians' work is evolving, including the importance of diversifying the ways librarians support the curriculum and ILI. After evaluating the literature, Johnson (2018) concludes,

> It seems imperative if reference and liaison librarians are to remain vital to their academic mission, that they find a way to look beyond 'sufficiently embedded' to explore what it might look like if they were to inextricably link themselves to the research and teaching enterprise in a systematic way. (p.98)

It may not be enough for liaison librarians to continue doing what they've always done but instead look to new ways to support students and faculty, in ways that tie them more closely to the institution's curriculum.

Similarly, a literature review by Cox (2018) highlights the changes within higher education and the ways in which librarians are shifting their work and roles to better align with their institutions' goals. It is important for librarians to position their library's strategies within the institution's overall strategies and mission. This allows library staff to focus on users over collections and developing wider partnerships on campuses re-center the library on campus in new ways. Choosing to position the library in new ways keeps librarians and their work relevant to their institutions.

As the academic landscape changes, it follows that those changes also affect library instruction or information literacy coordinators and other library leadership. Library leaders need to find ways to help their teams stay up to date with changes in higher education, including curricular changes and changes in instruction delivery mode. As institutions of higher education continue to grow and adapt the ways in which they provide education to students—particularly around online and asynchronous course delivery—librarians have the opportunity to create partnerships that result in new ways of providing ILI. Instruction coordinators will have the opportunity to lead their teams into new areas of promoting ILI, partnering with faculty, and finding ways to strategically place ILI into the curriculum. This chapter outlines how one university library is working to embed library instruction into the curriculum through faculty consultation on curriculum and discusses the importance of the role of a library instruction co-ordinator to help create a sustainable instruction program as part of the process.

Background

Concordia University, St. Paul (CSP) is in St. Paul, Minnesota. As of fall 2021, CSP has a full time equivalency (FTE) of just over 5,500 students, of which approximately two-thirds are online or distance students only. CSP has also seen steady enrollment growth over the past decade; for example, in 2011, CSP had fewer than 3,000 students. Much of the increase in enrollment comes from an increase in online or distance programs, particularly in health and business, but overall CSP programs range from undergraduate to graduate programs, across many disciplines, both on-campus and online. This creates unique opportunities for librarians to support information literacy instruction in a variety of settings and formats.

The CSP library employs eight total librarians, of which four, including the associate director for instruction and outreach, are part of the library's instruction and outreach team. This team focuses on providing instruction in courses, both in-person and asynchronously, staffing the Research Desk, as well as outreach to their assigned liaison areas. Each librarian is a liaison to at least one of the university's six academic colleges. Instruction and outreach librarians are also part of the university's Curriculum and Instruction Center (C&I Center).

The library director leads the C&I Center, and the center comprises a large part of the library staff's workload. The Center was created in 2018 at the direction of the university's provost, with the goal of helping faculty improve their online courses and curriculum. It is led by a cross-departmental team made up of instruction librarians, instructional designers, and IT Learning Management System (LMS) staff. Faculty meet with this team to discuss their classes, assignments, and other curricular needs, and to improve their courses. The staff from the C&I Center share an office space in the library and work closely on redesigning and consulting on courses. These new partnerships have dramatically changed both the work of the instruction librarians and the nature of the library's instruction program. Assisting with course designs and consulting with faculty has become the largest part of our job, allowing the library and instruction to be embedded directly into many courses.

Around the same time as the creation of the C&I Center, the CSP Library gained a new library director. The associate director for instruction and outreach position was also created in 2018. The associate director position is specifically responsible for overseeing and supervising the instruction and outreach librarians and the library's instruction program. Both personnel changes happened just before the creation of the C&I Center, providing more oversight of the librarians as they began their work in the C&I Center.

C&I Center Work

Work in the C&I Center focuses on two main curriculum-related tasks: designing or redesigning courses and programs, and providing course consultations. Designing or redesigning a course usually occurs within an entire program re-design, in which all courses in a program or major are redesigned. Both re-designing and designing a course from scratch generally involves a back-and-forth, several-months-long collaborative process among at least one faculty member (or course writer) who is the subject matter expert, instructional designers, and li-brarians. LMS staff are also included as needed to ensure the course will work properly in Blackboard, the campus LMS.

The redesign team examines courses piece by piece, reviewing discussion board prompts, assignments, required and supplemental readings and materials, assess-ment rubrics, and so on. Librarians and instructional designers make re-commendations based on best practices in ILI and instructional design, although faculty are not required to take all recommendations. This highly collaborative process results in more engaging classes for students, with the goal of increasing student success and retention within each class and across an entire program.

The C&I Center staff also consult with faculty on revising individual courses. This process is less involved than an entire course redesign but still covers many of the same topics. The C&I Center staff review a course in Blackboard and write a 2-page report with high-level recommendations on a course, allowing the faculty members to incorporate the feedback on their own time. This report covers in-structional design, library and information literacy, and Blackboard re-commendations. Feedback is given with the goal of increasing student success and ranges from increasing student engagement on discussion board prompts, to re-ducing textbook costs for students, to ways to use Blackboard more efficiently.

Faculty may choose to work with the C&I Center staff on a voluntary basis, or they may be asked by the university administration to work with the C&I Center. Courses and programs chosen for a course redesign or consult are often courses that have high withdrawal or failure rates. Faculty members who volunteer to work with the C&I Center generally want to find ways to improve their courses and increase student engagement and success. Since the start of the C&I Center, librarians and the center staff have worked on over 60 individual courses across the university's curriculum, from undergraduate to graduate programs.

During all course designs, redesigns, and consultations, librarians give re-commendations on two major components of the course: textbook affordability or course materials, and research assignments and research skills. Librarians give basic copyright advice when faculty are choosing course materials. Additionally, being at the table when a course is being designed or redesigned allows the librarian to make recommendations on library instruction that may be helpful for the course. These recommendations are seamlessly embedded or built directly into the course.

For example, when a faculty member works with the instructional designer to create a new research assignment, the librarian is part of the process to discuss potential pain points students may encounter in the assignment or when conducting research. The librarian is also able to offer suggestions for library resources that might be helpful to include or offer an asynchronous ILI option to ensure students get the help they need to complete the assignment. Because we most often work with faculty to redesign all the courses within a program, we can scaffold instruction and skills across multiple courses.

Likewise, when faculty are choosing their textbook during a course redesign or are interested in adding supplemental resources to the course, the librarian can offer copyright-compliant suggestions. These suggestions may be open educational resources (OER), library-licensed materials, or some combination of both. Although the faculty member always chooses the final inclusion of materials, the librarian can often offer suggestions for resources that save the student money. The librarian can also offer materials from the library's collections that faculty are not aware of. This work has resulted in many courses choosing a textbook-free option, where students have no textbook costs associated with taking the class.

CSP has a primary course philosophy; meaning when courses are created all sections of that course will generally use the same template, outline, assessments, learning objectives, course materials, and so on. Regardless of the instructor, students will have the same educational experience. This does not happen in every program but many. This means that the library's recommendations in the C&I Center are put into every section of a course, not just the ones taught by faculty who have used library services in the past. Library materials and ILI are embedded into many sections of courses each semester, increasing the library's reach to students.

CSP Library Instruction Program

As instruction librarians' work has shifted to more collaborative, course development work, having a cohesive and strategic ILI program has become even more important as well. This has ultimately resulted in a more strategic information literacy program for students. Prior to the C&I Center and the creation of the associate director role, librarians were responsible for all instruction and outreach within their liaison areas. There was some coordination among the instruction librarians but without an instruction coordinator, each librarian had a significant amount of autonomy without much guidance. This autonomy allowed librarians freedom to create relationships and develop instructional materials for their liaison areas; however, there was little cohesive strategy or standardization across the library. This resulted in potentially uneven workloads and a piecemeal approach to ILI and outreach, as well as inconsistent library experiences for students in different programs.

Since 2018, we have worked to standardize various pieces of ILI and chosen to adopt a broad definition of instruction. Having a broad definition of ILI allows us to consider all areas we provide instruction as part of our instruction program. We include everything from one-shot instruction to LibGuides, to our reference desk and chat, as part of our instruction program. We have intentionally chosen to include both synchronous and asynchronous options as part of our program in order to provide instruction in as many ways as possible. We also find that this broad definition helps keep our work more sustainable, as we are not relying on only one method of providing instruction, and allows us the flexibility to suggest a variety of forms of instruction when we are working with faculty on their courses.

We consider our Research Desk an instructional space for one-on-one instruction, and all librarians have shifts during the week, including the library director and technical services librarians. This lends to sustainability, so the instruction and outreach team does not burn out on desk shifts. It allows all librarians to interact with students and see how their work connects to student success. In addition, because students in all programs may reach out to the Research Desk, all librarians maintain a base level of understanding of many databases and library resources, regardless of the subject area. Expecting one librarian to be the only point of contact for all of the students in their liaison area seems overwhelming and unreasonable. A shared reference model enables us to support students and ensures that we are all grounded in a student-facing and student-centered mentality.

When it comes to our work with course designs, we often recommend that faculty use language in research assignments that encourages students to reach out to the library via the Research Desk if they need help finding sources. Course designs also include LibGuides with the reference chat embedded. Both of these approaches contribute to sustainable student support because we have an entire team ready to help them.

While traditional undergraduate students often still receive library instruction in a more traditional library 'one-shot' session, the courses designed by the C&I Center focus on CSP's online programs. These courses are primarily asynchronous and rarely involve live sessions with students. In these situations, librarians cannot provide a one-shot library session—online or otherwise—and instead are creatively thinking of alternative forms of instruction.

Instruction and outreach librarians provide instruction in asynchronous courses in a variety of ways. In 2018, we subscribed to Infobase's Credo Information Literacy-Core modules (InfoLit-Core). As CSP was dramatically increasing its online programs, we realized the importance of expanding our ILI options. At the same time as we started collaborating with the faculty C&I Center, we also recognized the need for ready-to-go information literacy modules, which could be recommended to faculty as we designed their courses. These modules can be embedded directly in Blackboard, to provide students with instruction on a number of information literacy concepts, from recognizing bias, to choosing keywords, to refining search results. The modules follow the ACRL Framework for Information Literacy for Higher Education.

The librarian suggests targeted modules when the course is being redesigned. Librarians make these specific recommendations based on the assignment and their knowledge of the program as a whole. Faculty are generally not given access to the entire suite of modules, so that the librarians can maintain an overall view of what modules are being used across the curriculum. We did not want the modules to get embedded in courses we were not aware of, risking students having to repeat too many modules when faculty in multiple courses picked the same modules. Instead, if a particular assignment focuses on peer-reviewed research, the librarian may suggest a video focused on explaining the peer-reviewed process and if another assignment focuses on APA, the librarian can suggest a tutorial focused on academic integrity and citation.

We also consider our LibGuides and video tutorials part of our instruction program. These additional asynchronous options provide classes with some basic library instruction, whether or not a librarian ever visits the class. Because we control the content on our LibGuides and in our videos, they are also more personalized than the InfoLit-Core modules. Again, when faculty reach out, we offer suggestions based on their assignment and learning outcomes, the same way we would with a one-shot instruction session. These suggestions often happen within the context of a C&I Center course redesign or consultation but have expanded to other programs as well.

For on-campus classes that do request one-shot instruction, instruction and outreach librarians are generally responsible for providing that instruction within their liaison areas. However, in order to better balance our workloads and support our on-campus students, everyone on the instruction team helps provide instruction to classes that are part of the general education required curriculum. This keeps one librarian from burning out on visiting all the introductory writing classes, for example, and allows the team to balance their workload. Additionally, it has helped the librarians standardize what is covered in each of these classes.

Finally, CSP instruction librarians have chosen not to offer any type of embedded librarian option, where a librarian is available within the LMS for a part or all of a semester to answer questions. Although we recognize that this practice could result in deeper information literacy understanding, with finite time we have not chosen this approach. In the past, we found it more time-consuming for individual librarians than we can commit, as our other work increases.

Expanded Work and Partnerships

In addition to shifting the library's instruction program to a broader definition and more asynchronous options, our work within the C&I Center has also resulted in new collaborations with many other departments and programs on campus. These new partnerships have resulted in embedding the library directly into the curriculum with programs we may not have directly worked with as part of our C&I Center work. Because of these partnerships, we often say we don't know where our 'library' work ends and our C&I Center work begins. Many faculty do not know either, as our work with the C&I Center has formalized the library's role as a curricular partner on campus. As we sit in meetings with faculty about a course redesign, the door often opens to conversations about other programs or other instruction-related and library-related topics.

For example, our librarian who is the liaison to the College of Education had the opportunity to work with two different masters-level education programs on textbook affordability initiatives. She helped the faculty and department chairs move the programs entirely textbook-free, saving students thousands of dollars each semester. Instead of having students buy traditional textbooks each semester for each class, faculty worked with the librarian to create curated course material lists for each class. The faculty offered topics and learning outcomes and the librarian helped find appropriate course material options, either OERs or electronic materials from within the library's collections. Adding articles and ebooks from the library's collections as some of the textbook replacement options also ensures that the library's collections are used effectively and in many courses.

While not directly related to instruction, textbook affordability projects—this one and others—afford the librarians a deeper understanding of the curriculum and deeper relationships with the faculty. The projects have opened the door to additional conversations about instruction. In this case, one of the education programs also switched to an asynchronous format at the same time as choosing to make courses textbook-free. Because of the work the librarian had done on textbook affordability, she was able to then have conversations about library instruction in asynchronous courses, consulting on specific assignments and research needs. She was also able to create an asynchronous LibGuide module to help students learn research skills needed for their class and program, which is directly part of the assignment and contributing to student success in the course.

While these opportunities may have eventually happened through the liaisons' outreach efforts, collaborations such as this one remind our team that the C&I Center has formalized and centered our role on campus as collaborators on curriculum development. Because of the official work we've done with specific programs in the C&I Center, faculty see the value brought by engaging with librarians on their curriculum questions. As we work with more programs, both officially part of the C&I Center and separately, word spreads among faculty and our curriculum work is increasingly becoming a larger part of our jobs.

Another partnership that has come out of our work with the C&I Center is our ability to help support Blackboard, the campus' Learning Management System. We work closely with the LMS IT staff, and all instruction and outreach librarians have administrative access to Blackboard. While not directly related to library instruction, having deeper access to the LMS provides instruction and outreach librarians with a myriad of ways to embed ILI in classes. When faculty want a LibGuide for a class or to use an InfoLit-Core module, we are able to go into Blackboard and embed the materials directly. If faculty ask for library instruction via Zoom, we can go to their course in Blackboard and join the Zoom session without the extra step of them emailing a link to us. Additionally, if we get reports of broken library links in a course, we can more easily troubleshoot by logging into the course ourselves. This curriculum partnership, again, results in a deeper understanding of the curriculum and deeper relationships with the faculty. We are able to provide better library instruction because we can more easily see the context for the instruction within the overall arc of the course.

A part of our broad definition of instruction has included our need to be intentional with our LibGuides. As we started working with courses in the C&I Center, it became apparent that we needed to coordinate and standardize the way we create LibGuides. The instruction team worked to create a new template for LibGuides based on best practices within the literature. After creating new templates, we reached out to faculty and now have LibGuides embedded into over 300 classes in Blackboard. These guides are simplified for each class, usually only one to two subpages, pointing students to only the resources they need in that class. They also include the library's proactive chat so students can get help from a librarian directly from their course in Blackboard. The guides allow us to reach students in many different programs, whether we speak to the class or not, and whether we work with a course in the C&I Center or not.

In addition, as our work has expanded in some areas due to the C&I Center, we have had to step back and reflect on what things we need to let go of. Which partnerships are we spending less time on? Which partnerships *should* we spend less time on? We choose to pay close attention to the enrollment numbers for various majors and programs as a way to guide these decisions. For example, our College of Humanities and Social Sciences has very few majors—our largest programs or majors are in the other academic colleges. Although the College of Humanities and Social Sciences still offers many of the university's required general education courses, due to this distribution of classes, we have chosen to focus our instruction and outreach efforts primarily on those general education courses and less on the humanities majors. This is, of course, not because The Humanities are not important, but that other programs, such as graduate education, criminal justice, business, and nursing have growing numbers of students and growing research needs. We must prioritize our time and following enrollment trends is one way to do so.

Role of the Instruction Coordinator in Curriculum Partnerships

In the CSP Library, the associate director for Instruction and Outreach serves as the instruction coordinator. This individual supervises and manages the instruction librarians and oversees the instruction program. Each instruction and outreach librarian has the opportunity to work with their liaison departments in ways that are best suited to the needs of the faculty and department but the role of the associate director, like most instruction coordinators, is to ensure the team is cohesive in their strategy. As the university grows, we see the need for co-ordination and consistency among the librarians. This applies to all our work, whether it is our LibGuide design or our approach to reference. Having one person lead the team, keeping an eye on the program holistically, has helped ensure the team is unified in their approaches to instruction across the disciplines.

On a day-to-day basis, this means ensuring the team is coordinated and communicating regularly. All instruction and outreach librarians have weekly meetings with the associate director to talk about their priorities and projects. This gives the associate director a birds-eye view of what everyone on the team is working on. This also ensures that everyone's projects fit within the overall goals of the instruction team, C&I Center, and library. The instruction team also has weekly meetings to discuss larger projects. These meetings are where things like LibGuide templates or instructions strategies can be discussed. Finally, the instruction team also attends regular meetings with the entire C&I Center staff, in which staff discuss current work on courses in order to identify themes across the courses and address any issues.

As the university grows, the librarians are supporting more students than even five years ago. This not only requires a significant amount of collaboration and coordination but also highlights the importance of sustainability in our work. The associate director is also responsible for making sure the work done by the instruction team is as sustainable as possible given that everyone has finite time. For example, the CSP Library instruction team has a philosophy that all guides and videos created should be as generic as possible in order to allow reuse whenever possible. We avoid making very many class-specific videos or tutorials to minimize the amount of time needed to maintain and update them. Even our embedded course LibGuides reuse content from other guides whenever possible. All librarians also follow the same LibGuide template to ensure students in all programs have a similar experience.

This does not mean we do not consider learning outcomes for asynchronous instruction (LibGuides, tutorials, videos), but that we look for ways to be efficient. As a liaison to an entire college, a librarian cannot create specific videos for every class. Instead, they are encouraged to think about which classes need more specialized library instruction and which do not, in order to find the balance between highly personalized library instruction and generalized modules, videos, or tutorials.

These conversations happen regularly in meetings with library leadership and as stated before, the library follows the enrollment of the university. As some programs grow and others shrink, we challenge ourselves to redefine which courses and programs we can or should focus on. Admittedly, these are hard things to think about—librarians want to promote ILI in all courses! But, in this case, having an instruction coordinator ensures that the team is moving in the same direction and that individual librarians are not caught up in projects that are not of strategic significance to the library or the C&I Center. This coordinator role helps librarians prioritize their goals, work, and collaborations, although C&I Center collaborations generally take priority. This work can look like a type of coaching: asking librarians many questions to help them think through their work. It can also look like more intentional feedback and direction.

Other roles of the associate director are to advocate for ILI in other venues, with library and university leadership. Regular meetings with other library department heads ensure teamwork across the library. It also involves ensuring that the team has the professional skills they need to complete their work. As the instruction and outreach librarians have become more involved in curriculum work, they also need skills to understand instructional design. Finally, the coordinator also provides regular training and communication for all the librarians who staff the Research Desk.

Ultimately, much of the information literacy coordinator role involves finding a balance between helping individual librarians embrace autonomy and ownership, and ensuring the team has a collective strategy. Finding this balance has helped CSP instruction and outreach librarians prioritize their time, standardize pieces of ILI across programs and ensure consistency where needed. Having an information literacy coordinator also ensures consistency across the library's information literacy program.

Application

Although not all academic libraries have formalized roles in curriculum development and design, there are still considerations that any librarian or instruction coordinator can consider when evaluating or considering collaborations with faculty on curriculum. The following questions are not designed to be prescriptive but rather exploratory questions for brainstorming new partnerships that might be considered within a different context.

Questions to Consider When Seeking Campus Collaborations

- Take stock: which departments are already partners with librarians?
- Look ahead: what have we learned from current partnerships we could apply to new partnerships on campus?
- Which programs on campus are a priority for the college or university?
- Which programs are growing on campus?
- Which programs or courses have high research and information literacy needs?
- Which faculty seem open to collaborating with the library?
- Which programs may we need to consider less outreach to? How do we prioritize which programs need library support the most, knowing that librarian time is finite?

Questions to Consider When Coordinating Instruction

- How can we think broadly about instruction to best meet the needs of our students?
- In expanding the reach of library and information literacy instruction, what job duties may need to shift or change to accommodate the changes?

- What practices or duties might we need to give up in order to focus on those that are more meaningful?
- What does sustainability look like for my team?
- How can we combine different types of library instruction (synchronous or asynchronous) in order to teach students the information literacy skills they need for a specific class or program?
- What are the overall goals of the instruction program? Is everyone moving toward those goals within their own projects, subject areas, and so on?

Conclusion

Collaborating with faculty across the curriculum can be both a challenging and exciting opportunity. Academic librarians are not strangers to working with faculty and collaborating on specific assignments, ensuring students receive ILI appropriate to their needs. CSP librarians have found that by engaging with faculty in many different programs, their place on campus as curriculum partners has grown. Although their work with the Curriculum and Instruction Center started with a few programs, the library's partnerships have grown to include many programs on campus, regardless of whether the faculty work with the C&I Center in a formalized way.

The work we have done through this center has increased not only our curricular partnerships on campus with faculty, but also our need to coordinate and collaborate among ourselves. The library is now integrated into many programs on campus and is better able to provide relevant resources and ILI for students. By embedding the library—specifically, materials and ILI—into curriculum development, the library is at the center of student success.

Finally, as we have increased our partnerships on campus, having a library staff member in the role of the instruction coordinator has been essential to oversight of the instruction program and ensures the team is moving in a strategic and cohesive way. Having someone who can champion information literacy and move teams in the same direction is incredibly important. And as CSP and other higher education institutions continue to move toward remote learning opportunities and asynchronous education, the library instruction coordinator role becomes even more important, helping instruction librarians engage with faculty on curriculum.

References

Brasley, S.S. (2008). Effective librarian and discipline faculty collaboration models for integrating information literacy into the fabric of an academic institution. *New Directions for Teaching & Learning, 2008*(114), 71–88. 10.1002/tl.318

Cox, J. (2018). Positioning the academic library within the institution: A literature review. *New Review of Academic Librarianship, 24*(3/4), 219–243. 10.1080/13614533.2018. 1466342

Farrell, R., & Badke, W. (2015). Situating information literacy in the disciplines. *Reference Services Review, 43*(2), 319–340. 10.1108/RSR-11-2014-0052

Johnson, A. (2018). Connections, conversations, and visibility: How the work of academic reference and liaison librarians is evolving. *Reference & User Services Quarterly, 58*(2), 91–102. 10.5860/rusq.58.2.6929

Moran, C., & Mulvihill, R. (2017) Finding the balance in online library instruction: Sustainable and personal. *Journal of Library & Information Services in Distance Learning, 11*(1-2), 13–24. 10.1080/1533290X.2016.1223964

6

THE RIGHT TOOLS FOR THE JOB: INTEGRATING A VARIETY OF INSTRUCTIONAL MODES INTO AN INFORMATION LITERACY PROGRAM[1]

Dani Brecher Cook

Introduction

Over the past twenty or so years, there has been an increasing focus within higher education on developing students' information literacy skills prior to graduation. Accrediting bodies, such as the Western Association of Schools and Colleges (WASC) Senior College and University Commission and the New England Commission of Higher Education, have incorporated information literacy as a core competency that they look to be measured in their evaluation process, leading to a greater demand for information literacy-related learning outcomes in courses and support from librarians to help achieve those outcomes (New England Commission of Higher Education, 2021; Saunders, 2007; WASC Senior College and University Commission, 2013). Historically, academic librarians have carved out a professional niche in teaching so-called 'one-shot' instruction, where they provide a one-time lecture or workshop in a credit-bearing course to teach research skills. While the jury is still out on the efficacy of such sessions, library departments have been feeling the pressure of increased demand for their expertise and time, with many instruction librarians reporting feelings of burnout, with overwork consistently a significant factor (Nardine, 2019; Wood et al., 2020). Most academic libraries are not in a growth phase in terms of hiring personnel (Wilder, 2018), so without a change in strategy, the dual pressures of increasing information literacy instruction and shrinking numbers of library workers who provide instruction and have teaching expertise will lead to increasing challenges.

From these constraints, however, can come the motivation to pursue new and high-impact instructional approaches that meet students' evolving needs, while preserving librarian time and well-being. At the University of California, Riverside (UC Riverside) Library, this was the challenge we faced: an increasing

DOI: 10.4324/9781003038634-10

demand for information literacy-related support for a growing student population with fewer library workers available to provide that labor and expertise.

For some time now, there has been significant debate about the efficacy and utility of the library one-shot, where a librarian visits a class in a guest-lecturer-style role and attempts to inculcate students with transferable information literacy skills within a defined period (e.g., Howard et al., 2014; Pagowsky, 2021; Portmann & Roush, 2004). As the one-shot has waned in popularity, its efficacy understood to be minimal, there has been a growing movement of library workers advocating for more robust collaboration with faculty in academic departments and a scaffolded approach to information literacy instruction across the undergraduate experience (Bowles-Terry & Donovan, 2016; Nalani Meulemans & Carr, 2013). Librarians have taken a variety of approaches to doing this, from integrating at multiple time-points in a course (e.g., Secovnie & Glisson, 2019) to embedding within the campus learning management system (LMS) (e.g., Daly, 2010). While these ideas have been percolating in the field for decades now, there is still not a consensus on the most efficacious way to build information literacy into a curriculum, though our work at UC Riverside was informed by all these efforts.

Establishing the Need

Since the late 1980s, UC Riverside librarians have collaborated with faculty in the College of Natural and Agricultural Sciences to provide library instruction to students enrolled in entry-level courses (Association of Research Libraries, 1986). Between the 1990s and 2017, when the Teaching and Learning Department in the Library was created, campus grew from 7,242 to 20,069 undergraduate students, almost tripling in size (University of California [UC] Riverside, 2021). This overall growth in campus size led to significant increases in enrollment in every department across campus, with STEM fields especially impacted. Where librarians in the 1980s worked with a handful of introductory chemistry sections each quarter, librarians in 2016 were offering library sessions in multiple classrooms from 8 in the morning to 9 in the evening, Monday through Friday, of the first week of almost every quarter. In 2017, the Teaching and Leaning Department comprised five full-time teaching librarians, one full-time staff member, and one director – me – who also did some teaching. Librarians from other departments in the library, including administrators, catalogers, and more, had to be enlisted to meet the need, delivering sessions from a shared script of course content. Each year, librarians would report entering the academic quarter exhausted, having worked split shifts to accommodate the need for chemistry course instruction throughout the day. Following the library sessions, students would complete a paper-based quiz, which reference and instruction librarians would then grade by hand (over 1,000 each quarter). Library instruction session learning outcomes were not tied to course content beyond providing an overview of how to use the *CRC Handbook of Chemistry and Physics* (Rumble, 2021) to find the weight of various metallic solids, which was required for a lab later in the quarter.

Directly following the intense week of chemistry-related courses, librarians would then pivot to providing instructional support for an introductory biology course, which had been supported since the 1990s. Support for these classes had also taken several different forms over the years, before settling into a consistent pattern. By 2015, students would complete an online tutorial through the Blackboard LMS that introduced them to the library catalog, basic database searching, citations, and academic integrity ("Achievement Acquired: Library Academy," 2015). At the end of the tutorial, students would receive a certificate of completion that they would then need to show at an hourlong in-person library session. Between 20 and 25 sessions would be offered each quarter, and students would sign up for the session that best fit their schedule. Students would sign in on a physical sign-in sheet, which would then be shared with the academic co-ordinator for the biology course, so students could receive credit for attendance.

These two courses, CHEM 1LA and BIOL 05LA, serve as gateway courses for students in STEM fields at UC Riverside. Almost all STEM majors are required to take CHEM 1LA, and all life sciences majors are required to take BIOL 05LA or its accelerated equivalent BIOL 020. CHEM 1LA is a required prerequisite for BIOL 05LA. With so many students required to take these courses, an inherent scaffolded structure, and a significant amount of library worker labor required to deliver instruction each quarter, these courses were clear priorities for closer examination of how we could deliver high-impact instruction that aligned with course outcomes, while limiting the amount of time required to deliver the instruction.

Additionally, the library had supported a freshman advising course for majors in the College of Agricultural and Natural Sciences (CNAS), NASC 093. As the university grew and there was an increasing focus on student success, the number of these courses increased by over 500% between 2011 and 2018, from approximately 20 sections each fall to almost 100. Individual course instructors would sometimes contact subject specialists to do a library orientation, but demand was unpredictable, and could range from between 3 and 10 sections every fall quarter, without any targeted outreach. Once again, if we wanted to provide a standard library introduction experience for CNAS, we ran up against the problem of scale – we couldn't expand efforts without significant growth in our workforce.

In conversation with librarians in both Teaching and Learning Services and Research Services, many of whom had worked with these classes for many years, we determined that working on a pathway through NASC 093, CHEM 01LA, and BIOL 05LA that maximized student learning and minimized synchronous staff time would benefit everyone involved. With a new Director of Teaching & Learning joining the UC Riverside Library in summer 2016, it felt like the right moment to revisit long-standing processes and practices.

(Re-)Building Relationships

The first step to creating changes in collaboration with these courses was to re-establish relationships with the course coordinators and determine mutual goals.

Since CHEM 01LA was the most labor-intensive of the three courses to work with, I decided to start the conversation there in fall 2016. I met with the co-ordinator of the course, and we discussed one of the major labor points first – the paper-based quiz at the end of the in-person session. Together, we determined that we would transition to a Qualtrics-based quiz, which would not only allow for automated grading but also allow us to easily see trends in student responses. Using the quiz, we were able to determine whether students were able to perform tasks related to the learning objectives of the library session, including finding materials in the library catalog, locating course reserves, and looking up chemical information in the *CRC Handbook of Chemistry and Physics*. We discovered that most students were not able to perform these tasks immediately after the library session, and it was anecdotally reported that students were not using the *CRC Handbook* in the lab session that required it.

Meanwhile, in Spring 2017, the new course coordinator of BIOL 05LA approached me and proposed that the learning outcomes for that course's library sessions be revised, based on feedback from students. Students from that course reported that they found the library sessions to be tedious and repetitive, and that they weren't able to apply most of what they were learning in the library sessions. This was not a complete surprise to me, as one day I had been standing outside a library classroom, waiting to prepare for a BIOL 05LA session, when a student came up to me and asked if we could go inside. "It will just be a minute, while the other class finishes up," I said. It soon became clear that the student mistook me for another student, when she said, "Got it. Well, I heard it's just going to be a waste of time anyway."

"Yikes, I hope not, since I'm the one who has to teach it!" I responded, and I invited her to give me feedback at the end of the session. If the word was out that the library sessions weren't a good use of student time, then it was definitely time for a change.

To first determine whether students were achieving the desired outcome of finding a scholarly journal article based on coverage in the popular media, librarians and the course coordinator collaboratively planned a research study to investigate whether students were more likely to demonstrate mastery of the outcome after the library session. We conducted two quarters' worth of data collection, which revealed that students were not more likely to find the article successfully after the library session, and that the number of students who changed their search behavior based on what was presented in the session was quite small. Gathering this data helped to establish the need for a change in both the library's and the academic program's instruction.

Finally, in late 2017, we began conversations with the lead advisor for the first-year student advising course, CNAS 093, to discuss how we could best support students entering UC Riverside for the first time. Affordability was a major component of that conversation, and the advisors specifically noted that students struggled without their course materials and were not aware of many academic library resources, such as course reserves. Because it is a required course for incoming students, developing a collaboration with CNAS 093 opened a possibility for getting students the logistical information about the library at the moment when they were learning how to be successful college students.

In order for us to even begin to have the internal conversation about how to re-imagine our approach to teaching entry-level courses in the natural sciences, we had to re-develop relationships and trust with the academic programs. A key part of this process was gathering specific data about how students were (and were not) meeting the desired learning outcomes of the course. In addition, we were able to work with the course coordinators to surface the ways in which the courses had changed over time. This understanding then allowed us to work together to create a shared understanding of the needs for change and agree to invest the time and resources into developing a plan that would be most likely to help students succeed.

Developing a Scaffolded and Multi-modal Curriculum

Rather than attempt to create stand-alone instructional solutions for each of these three natural science courses, we decided to intentionally design an information literacy-focused pathway through the courses, aligning learning outcomes and modalities with the specific moments that students would need and apply skills.

Determining the order of the pathway was relatively straightforward, as you can see in figure 6.1. Incoming first-year students were required to take NASC 093 in their first quarter, so that had to be the first stop. Next, all natural science majors were required to take the introductory chemistry sequence before they could advance to other courses, so CHEM 01LA made sense as the next touch point. Finally, students were asked to perform more complicated information literacy tasks in BIOL 05LA, so that became the final critical touchpoint on the CNAS information literacy path.

Before we could begin development, however, we needed to come up with an overarching learning outcome strategy, to ensure that there was a narrative through-line between all courses and that each course did indeed build on the last (see figure 6.2).

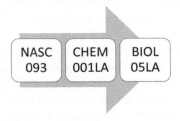

FIGURE 6.1 Introductory STEM courses pathway

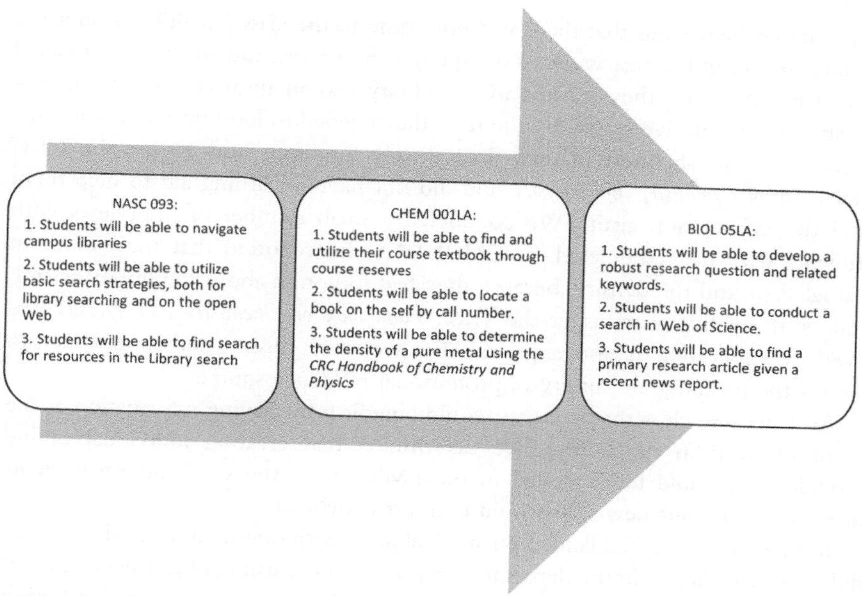

NASC 093:

1. Students will be able to navigate campus libraries

2. Students will be able to utilize basic search strategies, both for library searching and on the open Web

3. Students will be able to find search for resources in the Library search

CHEM 001LA:

1. Students will be able to find and utilize their course textbook through course reserves

2. Students will be able to locate a book on the self by call number.

3. Students will be able to determine the density of a pure metal using the *CRC Handbook of Chemistry and Physics*

BIOL 05LA:

1. Students will be able to develop a robust research question and related keywords.

2. Students will be able to conduct a search in Web of Science.

3. Students will be able to find a primary research article given a recent news report.

FIGURE 6.2 The learning pathway through the three courses, developed in consultation with the relevant academic department coordinators

CHEM 01LA: From All-in-One to Just-in-Time Instruction

Due to the significant labor of providing CHEM 01LA instruction each quarter, we decided to begin developing our pathway in the middle of the sequence. By removing both the scheduling and delivery of instruction stressors that recurred every ten weeks, we anticipated that we would have more time and mental energy to develop the other courses.

The transition to a self-grading Qualtrics-based quiz allowed us to rework the content to better align with current course outcomes. Each question was adapted from the original lesson plan for the course, including questions about call numbers, interlibrary loan, searching in two different catalogs, and the *CRC Handbook of Chemistry and Physics*. We maintained the original quiz's format, which provided multiple question options within each category of question, randomized across the quiz in order to prevent academic dishonesty (though we did eventually remove this practice and encouraged students in the class to work together). The move to Qualtrics opened up hours of grading time and allowed us to clearly see the questions that students continued to struggle with after the in-person library session.

One of our first steps in looking at each course was to think through the mode of delivery. While the CHEM 01LA classes were very labor intensive to offer in-person, we were open to continuing them if there were clear benefits to a mediated discussion. The academic coordinator for CHEM 01LA shared with us that one challenge was that there was only time in the class schedule to offer the library session in the first week of the quarter; however, students were not called on to use the skills they learned in the library session until conducting an experiment in week five or six. By the time they needed to look up the density of a metal for their lab, most of them had already forgotten how to use the *CRC Handbook of Chemistry and Physics*, and did not have a learning aid to help them find the information again. We conducted a small number of interviews with students who had completed CHEM 01LA, who reported that most of them Googled to find the density, because they had forgotten about the library session and/or the pathway to using the *CRC Handbook of Chemistry and Physics* was overly complicated. It also appeared that we were missing an opportunity to discuss the meaning and utility of professional reference sources.

As it became clear that students would benefit from having information at the point of need in the course, we determined that creating individual online modules that could be deployed in the LMS during the week before students needed to use their new skill would be most beneficial.

It seemed like we had landed on an ideal plan, with one significant hiccup: We didn't have someone in the department with a strong learning object development background and the time to devote to a project like this. Fortunately, in Spring 2018, UC Riverside's Undergraduate Education (UE) program put out a call for departments to propose meaningful summer learning and working experiences for students, which UE would co-fund for the summer. Thanks to this opportunity, Teaching and Learning was able to hire our first-ever student worker, a third-year neuroscience student with a talent for animation and an interest in education. The department director, Early Experience Teaching Librarian, and student worker worked closely together to learn how to use the Articulate Rise software and selectively develop in Articulate Storyline, which has a much higher learning curve.

During Summer 2018, we developed the first two modules: Finding Course Reserves (Yonezawa et al., 2021a) and Using Call Numbers (Yonezawa et al., 2021b). These two modules were meant to be completed at the beginning of the course, so that students would be able to find their course materials through the library. In developing these two modules, we solidified our approach to designing learning objects, focusing the opening of each module on the "so what" factor and creating a narrative that would resonate with the student experience. The student worker came up with the idea to use anthropomorphic blobs as characters who exemplify the experience of UC Riverside natural sciences students (see figure 6.3).

The student worker created the animation in PowerPoint, and we carried the characters through all of the Natural Sciences modules, to build continuity across the three courses.

The modules also included opportunities for students to practice using the skills described in the course, such as stepping through an interactive process of finding a course reserve, ordering call numbers, and finding a book. When students

FIGURE 6.3 An example of "the Atoms" setting the stage for the module learning outcomes, by struggling to find a copy of their course textbook. Used by permission of University of California, Riverside Library

completed the module, they received a completion grade in the LMS, negating the need for hand-grading or hand-inputting of Qualtrics scores. In conversation with the chemistry academic coordinator, we explored whether a differentiated grade would matter for these modules, and decided that having students complete the modules (and receive extra credit) would meet the course goals, as students have to correctly answer questions to complete the module.

By the end of the summer, we had run out of development time, so rather than rush to create the most complicated module on using the *CRC Handbook of Chemistry and Physics*, we created a two-page job aid PDF with step-by-step instructions for how to find the density of a pure metal. While this did not include the "so what" factor, it did help move us toward the development of the module by articulating the steps required to achieve the lab activity.

We launched the first two modules in fall 2018 and began to collect feedback from students on the modules to inform our future updates and development. Meanwhile, we began to work on the narrative for the final CHEM 01LA module, which would meet the learning outcome of students being able to look up and use the density of a specific pure metal in a laboratory experiment. As can be seen in figure 6.4, we first developed sub-learning goals and then drafted out a narrative pathway through the module.

From our interviews with students, we learned that many were unsure about why they needed to be able to look up statistics about metals and elements. Because of this feedback, we spent considerable time iterating and gathering input on whether the rationale was compelling and clear. Since we knew that many students turned to Google to complete their experiment, with a variety of results,

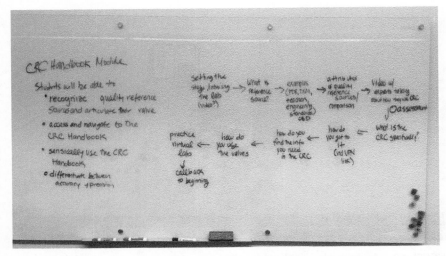

FIGURE 6.4   Outline for the *CRC Handbook* module. Photograph by the author

we built our explanation around that common behavior, as can be seen in figures 6.5 and 6.6.

By fall 2018, we launched the final CHEM 01LA module, and began development on the re-imagined BIOL 05LA.

Common Reference Sources

Experts consult specialized reference sources all the time, when they need to look up information related to their work. For example:

- Physicians use the PDR (Prescribers' Digital Reference) to find up-to-date information on dosages, side effects, and interactions of different medications.

- Engineers refer to standards to make sure that their systems, products, and processes meet professionally agreed-upon criteria.

- Psychiatrists use the DSM-5 (Diagnostic and Statistical Manual of Mental Disorders) to determine how to diagnose their patients, based on symptoms.

FIGURE 6.5   A screenshot from the CHEM 01LA tutorial demonstrating common reference sources. Used by permission of the University of California, Riverside Library

Why should you use it?

If you Google search for gold's boiling point, you find various values. The first three values found in a search for gold's boiling point are shown below.

	Google Search Result	ChemicalElements.com	Gold Traders Site	CRC Handbook
Boiling point of gold	2700 °C	2807 °C	2856 °C	2836 °C

With all of this variety in values, how will you know which one you can trust?

In an experimental setting, a constant that is incorrect by a few degrees or grams can result in inaccurate measurements, false results, or even a miscalculation that leads to an explosion or other dangerous outcome.

As the sciences continue to advance, the CRC Handbook periodically updates its data by adding new information and ensuring the accuracy of their numbers. Each year, experts carefully review new values and constantly strive to improve the usability of the CRC Handbook, making it a quality reference source that students can depend on.

FIGURE 6.6 A screenshot demonstrating the importance of reliable reference sources. Used by permission of the University of California, Riverside Library

BIOL 05LA: Teaching Students to "Think Like a Scientist"

For several years, BIOL 05LA's information literacy sessions had consisted of both an online and in-person component. The original online component was wide-ranging, covering topics from how to navigate Academic Search Complete to avoiding plagiarism. The in-person session then reiterated some of the same topics, including a live demonstration of searching Web of Science and Academic Search Complete.

As we sat down to plan how to approach the course, we identified from our study that one of the most significant pain points for students was how to accurately identify a primary research article. Their assignment asked them to find a primary research article based on a news source given to them by their teaching assistant (TA), yet many of them wound up identifying another news source or a campus press release rather than the original scholarly article. This seemed to be a complex topic, that could warrant a 50-minute guided discussion, while the basics of searching could perhaps be relegated to the online pre-work. In this case, we decided to take a multi-modal approach, employing an Articulate Rise-created module to give background information and procedural knowledge, and then use an in-person class session to practice the task that they would be asked to perform on their own as part of the CREATE-style (Consider, Read, Elucidate hypotheses, Analyze and interpret data, Think of the next Experiment) assignment (Hoskins et al., 2011). Because of the success and labor-savings of the CHEM 01LA development, we were able to advocate for consistent library funding for a student instructional design position, so our talented student designer was able to join us in developing this module as well.

Once again, we began our development process focused on the "so what" – what were the goals of the CREATE assignment, and why should students care? We wanted to make the implicit goals of the sequence explicit to the students. From the BIOL 05LA academic coordinator, we learned that the main goal of the course was to get students to "think like scientists," critically analyzing data, utilizing the scientific method, and identifying the appropriate evidence for a scientific claim. That message became the theme of the online module portion of the course: "Thinking Like a Scientist" (Ung et al., 2021).

The module sets the stage for the "why" in an initial animated section, once again featuring the Atoms, as can be seen in figure 6.7.

The module introduces the concept of doing background research as part of the scientific method, building on previous evidence and knowledge. Students complete exercises related to creating robust research questions, developing relevant keywords, and using Web of Science and other academic databases. The tutorial explicitly sets up the conversation for the in-person session, during which students practice identifying keywords from a news source, using an academic database to find the original primary research article, and successfully identifying the *correct* primary research article.[2] Once again, we were able to integrate the

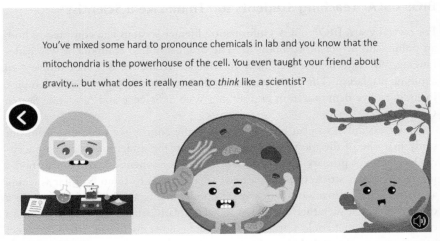

You've mixed some hard to pronounce chemicals in lab and you know that the mitochondria is the powerhouse of the cell. You even taught your friend about gravity... but what does it really mean to *think* like a scientist?

FIGURE 6.7 A screenshot from the BIOL 05LA module introducing the concept of "thinking like a scientist." Used by permission of the University of California, Riverside Library

module into the LMS, so that students would automatically receive a simple completion grade.

To make the most of the in-person sessions, the Early Experience Teaching Librarian carefully created a lesson plan that mirrored the experience of "Thinking Like a Scientist" and the CREATE assignment, finding a recent news article on a timely topic and then having students work together individually or in small groups to practice the skills of keyword development, searching, and article identification with expert feedback. During the session, students were asked to perform the task twice, with the results captured in a Qualtrics form. This allowed us to see whether there was a progression in skill between the beginning and the end of the class. By having students sign into the Qualtrics form, we also could generate a spreadsheet noting which students had completed the in-person session. This streamlined our previous attendance process that had required librarians to enter data from hand-signed roster sheets into the LMS grading system. We fully launched the new approach to teaching for BIOL 05LA in fall 2019, at the same time as the new NASC 093 approach, which is described in the following section.

NASC 093: Creating Bite-Sized Basic Modules

The final piece of our instructional pathway was the college skills focused NASC 093 course. While we had historically only worked with a handful of sections each fall, those numbers were growing, and we had the potential to reach all 100+ sections offered to first-year students. This course also had the potential for being a CHEM 01LA situation all over again, with every available library employee being asked to contribute to the teaching of basic library skills to an overwhelming number of students in a short period of time. By planning a scalable solution, we could both create consistency across sections and reach large numbers of incoming students without burning out library staff.

The size constraints led us to immediately consider a reusable online module solution. However, because there are so many sections of the course and significant limitations on our campus LMS, we could not embed a copy in each section. We decided to reimagine a previous solution from the original BIOL 05LA online module: Create a single site for students to navigate to, and auto-generate certificates of completion with their names for them to take screenshots and submit to their course instructor for credit.

To determine the learning outcomes, we examined what most librarians who had taught NASC 093 had been asked to cover by instructors, as well as student survey results on what they wished that they knew about the library when they started college. To that end, we focused the modules on the basics of access:

- how to connect to the campus VPN in order to utilize Library resources,
- how to navigate the library website,
- what services are available in each campus library, and
- the basics of searching.

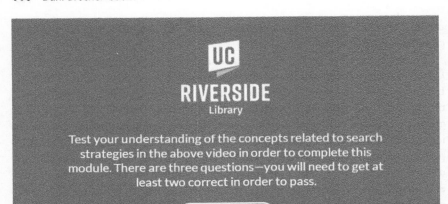

FIGURE 6.8 NASC modules required students to successfully complete a short quiz. Used by permission of the University of California, Riverside Library

Since most students would either be co-enrolled with CHEM 01LA or take it soon after NASC 093, we did not include information about course reserves. Discipline-focused teaching librarians contributed short videos to the modules, including closed captioning, as well as textual content. A short quiz at the end of each sub-module was required before students could receive their completion certificate, as seen in figure 6.8.

In fall 2019, we initiated a soft launch of the module for NASC 093 course instructors who requested library instruction; all but one agreed to try out the modules instead of having an in-person session.

Evaluation and Iteration

Updating modules to keep up with course, technology, and student learning changes is labor-intensive, and we did not want the module content to become stale, so we decided to schedule maintenance each summer. For example, in summer 2021, the UC Libraries system had a major system migration, so all of our modules required an update. Since we had already scheduled that into our workflow and developed documentation for student workers to follow, it was reasonably straightforward to make those changes.

Additionally, each course has satisfaction-focused evaluations built into them. At the end of each session, students are asked if they would recommend the module to a fellow student, and what they liked least and best. Most students have shared that they enjoy the modules, find them engaging, and especially love the Atoms. Some of the most interesting early responses came from students who were repeating a course and had encountered the previous iteration of instruction; universally, they preferred the new method. We frequently read and examine this feedback and have used it to identify when we can make explanations clearer or improve an activity.

One challenge of the way that these modules are deployed through the LMS is that we are not able to capture where students are struggling in the modules – we only can see the pass/fail rate. In the future, we hope that we can integrate the modules so that we can see a more granular view of where students might need additional clarity or support. If this is not possible, then user studies in which we observe participants going through the modules may also help us to refine these tools.

For the synchronous BIOL 05LA class, we can measure student progress within the 50-minute class via the Qualtrics survey. This helps us to determine if students are growing in their skills during the class, and checks that identifying primary source articles is still a skill they need help with via the pre-test.

Finally, we are aware that certain examples and language may not age well with time. One of the rationales behind creating the Atoms was that their outfits (which are non-existent) won't freeze them in time the same way stock photos would, so we did build some of those considerations into the design. However, just like we look for system changes each summer, we revisit the language and examples, and specifically refresh the BIOL 05LA examples annually, if not more often. We also make sure to stay in contact with the academic coordinators each quarter, to check in on their macro-level perspective and adjust to any curricular changes.

Next Steps

Though the pandemic was unanticipated, we were fortunate to have completed and launched our new Natural Sciences information literacy pathway prior to its beginning. This allowed us to smoothly pivot to delivering all instruction online, since the only course that still required an in-person, discussion-based component was the more advanced BIOL 05LA. We were able to transition that instruction to Zoom and utilize breakout groups, as well as host larger sessions, since we were not bound by classroom size. It is likely that we will continue to offer a Zoom option to students in the future, as more people are comfortable with the technology and may not be on campus every day.

This information literacy pathway for STEM also provides the backbone for thinking through other major opportunities at UC Riverside. For example, the Early Experience Teaching Librarian recently led an effort to adapt the BIOL 05LA "Thinking Like a Scientist" module for psychology (Yonezawa et al., 2021). This module will replace another labor-intensive introductory course, allow students to go back and review information shared, and provide instructional space for discussing challenging information literacy concepts in upper-division classes. The flexibility of the design of the modules means that they can continue to be adapted and iterated, both at UC Riverside and beyond.

By considering alternate approaches to course-related instruction beyond the traditional in-person (or Zoom) one-shot, we were able to both create space for instruction librarians to spend time in courses where that in-person component may have a more significant impact, and to ensure that students were receiving content that was both relevant and timely to them. It should not be assumed that in-person, synchronous instruction is always the best method. Most instruction programs are not growing in personnel, so it will be critical moving forward to consider where significant up-front investments can be made to maintain the quality and depth of instruction that programs may have previously provided with significantly more staffing. This also means that instruction departments will need to grow or hire people with skillsets in instructional design. By no means is this a new call for instruction programs to acquire these skills, but the need continues to grow. Effective instruction programs need to be able to provide high-quality, meaningful instruction in a variety of modalities, while maintaining a consistent and reasonable workload for library workers. A mixed modality instruction program opens the door to that possibility.

Notes

1 With gratitude to the members of the UC Riverside Library Teaching & Learning Department, without whom none of this work would have been possible: Christina Cicchetti, Kenneth Furuta, Judy Lee, Christopher Martone, Robin Katz, Phyllis Ung, Michael Yonezawa, and honorary member David Rios. And to our campus partners: Star Lee, Kevin Simpson, and the CNAS Academic Advising Center.
2 For more on the development of the tutorial, please see Maniates, 2021.

References

Achievement acquired: Library academy. (2015, July). [Newsletter]. *UCR Library Newsletter.* https://us10.campaign-archive.com/?u=3d3292965cebf17f0755f5ae2&id=73830a3a10

Association of Research Libraries. Systems and Procedures Exchange Center. (1986). *Bibliographic instruction in ARL libraries.* Association of Research Libraries, Office of Management Studies. https://catalog.hathitrust.org/Record/000661875

Bowles-Terry, M., & Donovan, C. (2016). Serving notice on the one-shot: Changing roles for instruction librarians. *International Information & Library Review*, 48(2), 137–142. 10.1080/10572317.2016.1176457

Daly, E. (2010). Embedding library resources into learning management systems: A way to reach Duke undergrads at their points of need. *College & Research Libraries News.* 10.5860/crln.71.4.8358

Hoskins, S.G., Lopatto, D., & Stevens, L.M. (2011). The C.R.E.A.T.E. approach to primary literature shifts undergraduates' self-assessed ability to read and analyze journal articles, attitudes about science, and epistemological beliefs. *CBE Life Sciences Education*, 10(4), 368–378. 10.1187/cbe.11-03-0027

Howard, K., Nicholas, T., Hayes, T., & Appelt, C.W. (2014). Evaluating one-shot library sessions: Impact on the quality and diversity of student source use. *Community & Junior College Libraries*, 20(1–2), 27–38. 10.1080/02763915.2014.1009749

Maniates, R. (2021, April). *PRIMO site of the month interview: April 2021: Thinking like a scientist.* ACRL Instruction Section. https://acrl.ala.org/IS/instruction-tools-resources-2/pedagogy/primo-peer-reviewed-instruction-materials-online/primo-site-of-the-month/primo-site-of-the-month-interview-april-2021/

Nalani Meulemans, Y., & Carr, A. (2013). Not at your service: Building genuine faculty-librarian partnerships. *Reference Services Review, 41*(1), 80–90. 10.1108/00907321311300893

Nardine, J. (2019). The state of academic liaison librarian burnout in ARL libraries in the United States. *College & Research Libraries, 80*(4), 508–524. 10.5860/crl.80.4.508

New England Commission of Higher Education. (2021). *Standards for accreditation.* https://www.neche.org/resources/standards-for-accreditation/

Pagowsky, N. (2021). The contested one-shot: Deconstructing power structures to imagine new futures. *College & Research Libraries, 82*(3), 300–309. 10.5860/crl.82.3.300

Portmann, C.A., & Roush, A.J. (2004). Assessing the effects of library instruction. *The Journal of Academic Librarianship, 30*(6), 461–465. 10.1016/j.acalib.2004.07.004

Rumble, J. (Ed.). (2021). *CRC handbook of chemistry and physics* (102nd ed.). CRC Press.

Saunders, L. (2007). Regional accreditation organizations' treatment of information literacy: Definitions, collaboration, and assessment. *The Journal of Academic Librarianship, 33*(3), 317–326. 10.1016/j.acalib.2007.01.009

Secovnie, K.O., & Glisson, L. (2019). Scaffolding a librarian into your course: An assessment of a research-based model for online instruction. *Teaching English in the Two Year College, 47*(2), 119–148.

Ung, P., Yonezawa, M., Lee, S., & Cook, D.B. (2021). *Bio 05LA: Thinking like a scientist.* UCR Library teaching and learning objects. https://ucrlibraryteachingandlearning.github.io/learningobjects/bio_05La_forweb/content/index.html#/

University of California, Riverside, Institutional Research. (2021). *Enrollments: UCR.* University of California, Riverside. https://ir.ucr.edu/stats/enroll/overall

WASC Senior College and University Commission. (2013). *Standard 2: Achieving educational objectives through core functions.* 2013 Handbook of Accreditation. Retrieved August 16, 2021, from https://www.wscuc.org/resources/handbook-accreditation-2013/part-ii-core-commitments-and-standards-accreditation/wasc-standards-accreditation-2013/standard-2-achieving-educational-objectives-through-core-functions

Wilder, S. (2018). Hiring and staffing trends in ARL libraries. *Research Library Issues, 295*, 17–31. 10.29242/rli.295.3

Wood, B.A., Guimaraes, A.B., Holm, C.E., Hayes, S.W., & Brooks, K.R. (2020). Academic librarian burnout: A survey using the Copenhagen Burnout Inventory (CBI). *Journal of Library Administration, 60*(5), 512–531. 10.1080/01930826.2020.1729622

Yonezawa, M., Katz, R., Ung, P., & Frazier, D. (2021). *Thinking like a scientist (psychology edition).* UCR Library teaching and learning objects. https://ucrlibraryteachingandlearning.github.io/learningobjects/psyc12_forweb/content/index.html#/

Yonezawa, M., Ung, P., & Cook, D.B. (2021a). *CHEM 01LA module 1: Course reserves.* UCR Library teaching and learning objects. https://ucrlibraryteachingandlearning.github.io/learningobjects/chem1LA_module1/content/index.html#/

Yonezawa, M., Ung, P., & Cook, D.B. (2021b). *CHEM 01LA module 2: Call numbers.* UCR Library teaching and learning objects. https://ucrlibraryteachingandlearning.github.io/learningobjects/chem1LA_module2/content/index.html#/

PART IV
Meaningful Assessment

7

IMPROVING INFORMATION LITERACY INSTRUCTION THROUGH PROGRAMMATIC STUDENT LEARNING ASSESSMENT

Maoria J. Kirker and Ashley Blinstrub

Introduction

Student learning assessment follows a cycle of writing learning outcomes, collecting evidence of student learning, and revising instruction to improve learning. The implementation of a systemic student learning assessment plan in a library improves information literacy instruction through this iterative process.

This chapter will walk through the process of creating, implementing, and revising a student learning assessment plan in a large university library system. We will highlight major successes, setbacks, and lessons learned to help guide you wherever you may be in the assessment process. In doing so, we hope to illustrate the importance of collaboration, trust, patience, and humility in the assessment process. Creating a student learning assessment plan may sound like a daunting task, but we hope this chapter acts as a guide for beginning or modifying your student learning assessment plan to meet your needs.

Institutional Context

George Mason University (Mason) is a large, R1, public university in Northern Virginia. Mason has multiple campuses located across the Washington, DC, metropolitan area, but its main campus is a suburban campus in Fairfax, Virginia. In the fall of 2020, Mason enrolled approximately 23,300 undergraduate full-time equivalent (FTE) students and 29,600 total FTE students. Most students at Mason are from historically excluded populations.

The University Libraries comprises three major divisions. Most of the library instructors, both faculty librarians and classified staff, work in Learning, Research and Engagement (LRE). The units within LRE include Collections Strategy, the Special Collections Research Center, and four subject area teams: Arts and

DOI: 10.4324/9781003038634-12

Humanities, Science and Technology, Social Sciences, and Teaching and Learning. The Teaching and Learning Team focuses on teaching information literacy in large-enrollment, undergraduate, general education courses; the Arts and Humanities, Science and Technology, Social Sciences Teams teach information literacy in upper-level undergraduate courses in their disciplines and graduate programs.

The Student Learning Assessment Plan was developed by the Instruction and Assessment Coordinator on the Teaching and Learning Team. This position was later rewritten into two distinct roles: a student success and inclusion librarian, who oversees the Libraries' Student Learning Assessment Plan, and an instruction coordinator. These two positions collaborate with one another frequently to align instruction and assessment goals.

Depending on position vacancies, the number of library instructors fluctuates between 25 and 35 people with varying degrees of teaching and student learning assessment experience. Prior to the implementation of the initial Student Learning Assessment Plan in 2016, the University Libraries did not have any systematic student learning assessment. Some headway was made in 2013 with the Libraries' participation in the Association for College and Research Libraries' (ACRL's) Assessment in Action Program (American Library Association, 2012), and by 2014, there was a desire from University Libraries administration and key partners across Mason to measure student learning in the Libraries.

Developing the Original Student Learning Assessment Plan

When beginning any process of developing a culture of student learning assessment, library instructors need a place to start, but that starting point does not require novelty. At Mason, the first hurdle to overcome was integrating assessment into regular instructional practices. To accomplish this, library instructors developed a standardized one-minute paper, which required students to answer open-ended prompts about the session, at the end of the library instruction. The prompts on this assessment included:

- Describe the most useful concept or skill you learned in today's library session and how you would apply it.
- Do you have any remaining or new questions after today's library session?
- If you would like your question answered by the librarian, please provide your email.

While these questions are broad, the implementation of this half-page assessment helped build a habit of assessing learning by requiring library instructors to incorporate time into their lessons for assessment and to reflect on the responses after the session. A more targeted, outcomes-based assessment would follow once the Student Learning Assessment Plan was finalized.

Library instructors used this assessment for about a year (Spring 2015–Spring 2016). After collecting student responses and reviewing them individually, library instructors submitted their one-minute papers to the Instruction and Assessment Coordinator for collective analysis. These assessments did not address specific learning outcomes; they only provided limited evidence of student learning. However, the assessments did provide a snapshot of what library instructors taught (Kirker, 2016). This data helped inform the creation of the Libraries' initial student learning outcomes.

Building the Student Learning Assessment Plan around shared student learning outcomes was vital to create a way to measure student learning in library instruction. Development of the initial learning outcomes began the summer we implemented the one-minute papers. A previous iteration of the Teaching and Learning Team held a full-day professional development event in May 2015 called the "Instruction Forum," which focused on developing a shared understanding of what the unit teaches. Through the work completed this day and the weeks that followed, the unit wrote a shared teaching philosophy and six learning outcomes based on information literacy instruction in Mason's large-enrollment, undergraduate courses. The team piloted these outcomes during the fall 2015 semester. Based on the success of incorporating the outcomes, the Instruction and Assessment Coordinator presented the outcomes to all Mason library instructors in the spring of 2016 for library-wide adoption. There was overwhelming consensus for adopting the outcomes, and thus they became a part of the initial Student Learning Assessment Plan.

Structure of the Student Learning Assessment Plan

Meanwhile, the instruction and assessment coordinator attended the ACRL Immersion Program's Assessment Track in the fall of 2015. This professional development experience afforded the time and resources necessary to draft an assessment plan. The focus of the program was not exclusively on student learning; however, the instruction and assessment coordinator attended with the goal of producing a student learning assessment plan. The resources, tools, and expertise provided by the facilitators of the Immersion Program influenced the creation of the initial plan at Mason, which was adapted from assessment plan examples provided during the program (Bowles-Terry et al., 2015).

The Student Learning Assessment Plan is available to view on the Teaching and Learning Team's website (George Mason University Libraries, n.d.). Here, we describe each of the elements from the initial Student Learning Assessment Plan at Mason.

Purpose

The Student Learning Assessment Plan begins with a clear statement of what the plan is and is not. The plan states that the student learning assessment data will be used to improve student learning; inform and improve instructional practices; and strengthen the University Libraries' instruction initiatives. In foregrounding and emphasizing these elements, the intention is to illustrate that student learning assessment results will not be used as part of individual performance evaluations. Instead, assessment data will be used to create a snapshot of how the University Libraries contributes to student learning at Mason.

When developing the initial plan, piloting assessment through one-minute papers, and through multiple conversations with library instructors, it was clear that library instructors feared how the assessment data would be used. The purpose section of an assessment plan can mitigate some of these fears. To be successful with this, we recommend using clear and direct language that explicitly states what the plan does and does not accomplish.

Theory

Theoretical grounding for an assessment plan provides evidence-based support for the purpose statement. By adding a theoretical framework, libraries demonstrate how they connect educational, assessment, and motivational theories to their assessment processes (Oakleaf, 2010). Mason's assessment plan is based on Megan Oakleaf's work related to the Information Literacy Instruction Assessment Cycle (ILIAC) framework. The plan uses *assessment as learning to teach* as its theoretical framework, which is defined as "the practice of focusing on student learning goals and outcomes, assessing student attainment of learning outcomes, and implementing instructional changes to increase student learning" (Oakleaf, 2009, p. 541).

Strategic Connections

Connecting an assessment plan to related campus initiatives that impact student learning provides institutional context for an instruction program to embark on this type of assessment work. For the Mason Libraries' Student Learning Assessment Plan, these documents include Mason's *2014–2024 Strategic Plan* (George Mason University, 2013, p. 12), student learning assessment rubrics used across the university (George Mason University, 2014; George Mason Students as Scholars Initiative, 2016), and reaccreditation guidelines from the Southern Association of Colleges and Schools Commission on Colleges (SACSCOC) (Commission on Colleges of the Southern Association of Colleges and Schools, 2012). Additionally, we point to ACRL's "Framework for Information Literacy in Higher Education" as a foundational document informing the Plan.

Structures

Structure refers to campus offices that support assessment work. This includes data collection, analysis, and dissemination. The Student Learning Assessment Plan also includes a statement of support from library administration and outlines what position oversees and manages the plan.

Resources

If there are resources available, particularly monetary, highlight those resources. George Mason University Libraries could not guarantee financial resources for student learning assessment. The plan makes this clear. Assessment without participant compensation became an expectation, but at least one assessment project received funding during the initial three-year assessment cycle to compensate participants.

Data Policies

The initial Student Learning Assessment Plan's data policies section included information on gathering, storing, accessing, and reporting data. This section was developed in consultation with the University Libraries' Data Services unit. It outlined how librarians should provide the raw assessment data to the instruction and assessment coordinator. In practice, this section was the least followed in the plan – both by library instructors and the instruction and assessment coordinator. The revision of the Student Learning Assessment Plan, described later in this chapter, included more detail and flexibility for data management.

Outcomes

The original Student Learning Assessment Plan included six learning outcomes:

1. Students navigate the complex information landscape in order to locate information.
2. Students evaluate a knowledge source to determine its suitability for their information need.
3. Students identify multiple knowledge sources in order to compare, contrast, and synthesize diverse perspectives.
4. Students will seek out evidence to inform challenging decisions while developing an open-minded approach to inquiry.
5. Students recognize how political, social, economic, and professional contexts shape knowledge sources in order to engage in scholarly conversation within and across disciplines.
6. Students will recognize that the library's value exceeds traditional information sources in order to transfer their knowledge to experiences beyond the classroom.

These outcomes were to provide an overarching portrait of the skills and concepts the University Libraries wishes to teach in our information literacy instruction.

There was not an expectation that library instructors teach to every outcome in every instructional session. Additionally, if library instructors determined that none of the outcomes applied to an instructional context, they were not required to adapt their teaching to include the outcomes. Instead, the expectation was that each year library instructors completed a report on student learning based on one of two outcomes focused on for that year (refer to the section "Timeline for Continuous Improvement" for more information on this cycle). Reports could analyze student learning in a one-shot session, an embedded librarian experience, or multiple sections of the same course.

One piece of feedback from library instructors was that the outcomes felt too large or abstract. Based on this, a set of sub-outcomes was created. These sub-outcomes were designed to provide more concrete language. While the intention of the original six outcomes was for them to be large-scale, umbrella outcomes, some library instructors struggled with that concept.

Here is one set of sub-outcomes as an example:

- Outcome 4: Students will seek out evidence to inform challenging decisions while developing an open-minded approach to inquiry.
    - Students conduct multiple searches using divergent (e.g., brainstorming) and convergent (e.g., selecting the best sources) thinking.
    - Students analyze a topic or research question to determine whether a single answer or multiple, conflicting answers exist.
    - Students reformulate research questions based on information gaps and possibly conflicting information.

After these sub-outcomes were shared with library instructors, many indicated they felt more comfortable mapping the learning outcomes they used to teach to the broader outcomes in the plan.

Timeline for Continuous Improvement

The final section of the Student Learning Assessment Plan was a calendar for a three-year assessment cycle. From academic years 2017 through 2019, two outcomes would be assessed each year. The two outcomes were paired each year to have one outcome that was deemed easier to assess with a more difficult-to-assess outcome. This ultimately proved problematic, as assessment reports often only focused on the "easier" outcome.

Library instructors were asked to submit an annual assessment report detailing evidence related to one of the two annual outcomes. A report template and a sample report were provided to library instructors to help them write their own. Team and collaborative reports were also encouraged.

Implementation of the Original Student Learning Assessment Plan

The implementation of the Student Learning Assessment Plan generally went smoothly. Some challenges emerged throughout the process, such as insufficient training and resources for librarians; difficulties closing the assessment loop; and institutional culture challenges. These issues are explored in this section, alongside the successes that occurred, to paint a full picture of the complexities of implementing a student learning assessment plan.

Feedback and Training

In addition to the meetings for feedback and input on the creation of the original Student Learning Assessment Plan, a variety of other opportunities to provide feedback and answer questions happened in the months preceding its implementation. Throughout the summer before the implementation of the plan, the instruction and assessment coordinator met with each of the University Libraries' subject teams to enable these librarians to ask questions and to articulate their concerns about the plan. Most concerns centered on how the data collected would be used, to whom the assessment reports would go, and what would result from a "bad" assessment report. In this context, "bad" referred to a report that did not show evidence of student learning or revealed a poorly designed assessment.

What emerged from these meetings was a necessity to meet with library instructors one-on-one to set goals related to student learning assessment. One-on-one meetings provided a space for individuals to ask questions or raise concerns they did not feel comfortable doing in a group. The meetings also allowed for individualized goal setting. The individualization of these one-on-one meetings seemed to build trust among library instructors and ensure that the goal was not uniformity, but collective progress. These meetings continued throughout the first iteration of the Student Learning Assessment Plan, but participation significantly declined after the first year.

One-on-one meetings allowed for librarians to ask questions, but did not provide a continuous system of support throughout the assessment process. Well-timed trainings on student learning assessment and using the Student Learning Assessment Plan throughout the academic year might have aided with this; however, no such trainings occurred due to time constraints, shifting priorities over the three years, and staffing changes in the University Libraries. An assessment toolkit could have helped librarians. The toolkit would allow for librarians to use pre-made assessments or customize them to their instructional goals. Such a toolkit was not created for the initial Student Learning Assessment Plan but became a high priority during the revision process.

Assessment Data

One issue that became evident after the first year of the Student Learning Assessment Plan implementation was the disproportionate coverage of learning outcomes each year. Because the plan paired an easier-to-assess outcome with a more difficult one, librarians almost always assessed the easier outcome. In some ways this was anticipated; the instruction and assessment coordinator planned for a large-scale assessment on the more difficult outcome each year. Ultimately, this resulted in only one or two assessment reports for one of the two outcomes each year. This information was used in the revision process of the Student Learning Assessment Plan and informed whether one or both outcomes needed to be assessed each year.

Assessment reports also revealed librarians often confused student learning assessment data with patron satisfaction surveys. Instead of receiving reports that measured student leaning, some reports simply included data about whether students thought an information literacy session was useful, whether a LibGuide would be used in the future, and some quantitative data about how the library instructor could improve the session. Other reports did not approach their assessments from an outcomes-driven perspective; they continued using generic assessments like the one-minute paper. If these were connected to a learning outcome for the library session, it was not clearly reported. The instruction and assessment coordinator felt that lack of training related to student learning assessment was likely behind these types of reports.

The instruction and assessment coordinator compiled the assessment reports and used them to write a narrative of student learning for the University Libraries for George Mason University's Office of Institutional Effectiveness and Planning's internal reporting system. The narrative is used for reaffirmation with SACSCOC. Library instructors did not see this part of the process so there was confusion about what happened to the data from their assessment reports. Sharing out these final reports, which were anonymized and provided a snapshot of student learning in the University Libraries, might have alleviated this confusion. Additionally, because of reporting deadlines, each year a major assessment project did not make it into the report. This was due to the time commitment of large-scale, data-rich projects. The internal reporting system allows for revisions to reports; however, this complicated reporting out to library instructors.

Reception by Library Instructors

Library instructors understood the value and importance of the Student Learning Assessment Plan; however, the implementation of it was fraught. An institutional mandate from library administration to participate ensured that all library instructors assessed student learning and wrote an assessment report. This resulted in full participation, but it also built resentment about the assessment process. Confusion about the differences between assessment and instruction evaluation was part of this resentment. The instruction and assessment coordinator worked to build trust over multiple years and demonstrate how the assessment data would be used and, more importantly, how it would not be used. One example of this is sharing the annual internal report in order to show how data, course information, and instructor information were anonymized.

One part of the Student Learning Assessment Plan adversely received by some library instructors was the theoretical grounding in "assessment as learning to teach." Some perceived this as a slight, saying they already knew how to teach. Some interpreted this theory as an indication from the instruction and assessment coordinator and library administration that they believed library instructors did not know how to teach. This came as a surprise to the instruction and assessment coordinator, but this is likely related to an instruction evaluation process occurring simultaneously with the implementation of the Student Learning Assessment Plan.

Finally, as the initial three-year cycle of the Student Learning Assessment Plan concluded, many library instructors described an end of year report fatigue. Library instructors were required to write an assessment report, write an instructional self-evaluation, participate in a Teaching Square (Kirker et al., 2021), begin the annual evaluation process, as well as other types of documentation, all in May. There was a growing concern about why all of the reporting was needed and for what purpose. Clarifying the answers to these questions was necessary as the revision process for the Student Learning Assessment Plan began.

Review of the Student Learning Assessment Plan

An important step in a programmatic assessment is reviewing the assessment plan at the end of the cycle to ensure effectiveness and address any issues that arose during implementation. When beginning the revision process, it is important to look at how library instructors utilized the original document and what was learned from the data collected. If possible, discussions with the person who created the original plan to determine what they would have done differently can also be beneficial. During this time, Mason Libraries restructured the Teaching and Learning Team and hired a new Student Success and Inclusion Librarian who reviewed and revised the Student Learning Assessment Plan.

In approaching the University Libraries' Student Learning Assessment Plan, beginning with reviewing previous assessment reports provided valuable insights into how people used the plan and learned from their assessment projects. This review process revealed issues with trainings about student learning assessment and wording in the initial plan, and it informed future surveys and trainings for library instructors. This step in the process was also invaluable to editing and revising the student learning outcomes, as it revealed which of the outcomes were most assessed by library instructors. The review process also confirmed that library instructors often confused student learning assessment and instructional evaluation.

A formal survey of library instructors provided feedback about the initial plan. After reviewing the assessment reports, a targeted survey was developed for users of the assessment plan. Two important themes emerged from the survey results: marketing and training. Several users noted that they were not sure what to do with their data after the assessment process and did not know how to close the assessment loop. Library instructors were also very clear that they needed ideas of how to measure the learning outcomes. Additionally, there were some outcomes from the initial plan that users did not know how to assess. This echoed what the analysis of assessment reports revealed. However, gathering the survey data did give us specific reasons as to why certain learning outcomes were not assessed widely.

Talking to the creator of the initial plan provided valuable information in the revision process, including revealing issues with implementation of the first student learning assessment plan and changes in policies and titles since the creation of the plan. At the time of revision, the plan was four years old, and it was easier to learn about the policy changes from someone who had experienced them. Also, it was extremely helpful to learn more about what it was like to guide library instructors in their use of the plan and sticking points that arose. To ensure that this valuable information is not lost, annually reflecting on each section of an assessment plan and how it worked is recommended. Likewise, journaling or yearly documentation of issues, successes or revision ideas can be helpful when it is time to revise the plan. Taking the time to carefully review documentation, survey users, and think about the process for each iteration of the student learning assessment plan will lead to more effective plans.

Revised Student Learning Assessment Plan

The structure of the initial plan remained, but thoughtful changes to certain sections were made based on the data collected in the review process. The sections that needed the most revision were the learning outcomes and data policies sections. The purpose, theory, resources, and timeline all remained nearly identical in the revised plan. Some aspects of the plan needed simple updates, such as changing people's titles and department names. The strategic connections section also needed updates as there had been changes made to the university's strategic plan and SACSCOC in previous years.

Beginning these revisions thoughtfully and slowly made the process much smoother and led to a better end-product. It allowed feedback from both users of the initial plan and its creator. It was important not to completely revise every section of the plan since the process was carefully thought out in the initial plan. It is not always necessary to completely reinvent the wheel when updating a plan. Be strategic about the changes that need to be made. Focus on major points of confusion found in the review period when you begin revisions and ensure that you are updating your plan to align with any university policies that may have changed.

Outcomes

One of the biggest changes was developing new learning outcomes. The analysis of the initial plan revealed several difficulties library instructors had with the first set of outcomes. Firstly, one of the outcomes was not assessed by anyone that turned in an assessment report, "Students will recognize that the library's value exceeds traditional information sources in order to transfer their knowledge to experiences beyond the classroom." During the review period, it became apparent that this outcome was particularly difficult to assess in a one-shot library instruction classroom.

Another major change to the outcomes is the way they were paired in the assessment plan. In the initial plan, difficult outcomes were paired with easier outcomes. Library instructors were required to assess one outcome per year, which led to easier outcomes being assessed for student learning at a higher rate than the more complex outcomes. In the revised plan, outcomes were paired based on theme, to encourage a greater distribution of assessments. Library instructors also need to assess each of the outcomes annually in the revised plan.

Many new people joined the Teaching and Learning Team since the initial student learning outcomes were written, so a new, collaborative process was started to revise the learning outcomes. The team discussed directly tying the learning outcomes to the ACRL Framework for Information Literacy, which was more understood by the library instructor community in 2020 than in 2015. The team approach to creating these outcomes was helpful, but also included challenges. Hearing multiple people's perspectives on what would be useful for our community in learning outcomes was encouraging; however, narrowing specific language for six outcomes took longer than expected and resulted in multiple compound outcomes as everyone's ideas were considered.

With further revisions the team created six general outcomes that everyone agreed encompassed what is taught in library instruction classes. As with the initial plan, sub-outcomes were developed. The outcomes section of the plan also included directions for how to use them in teaching and assessment. During this process, library instructors were surveyed for their feedback about the new outcomes and a meeting was held to answer questions about them. The new outcomes are as follows:

1. Students will articulate their information need.
2. Students will locate resources using appropriate search tools and strategies for their information need.
3. Students will critically evaluate information and where it comes from.
4. Students will synthesize information from multiple sources.
5. Students will describe the information creation and dissemination process.
6. Students will identify the legal, economic, and social context of the use and creation of information.

These new outcomes guide the Student Learning Assessment Plan. As with the initial plan, sub-outcomes are useful because the six general outcomes are broad so that they encompass most disciplines. Library instructors were also encouraged to create their own sub-outcomes that related to the overarching outcomes.

It is recommended to spend a significant amount of time revising learning outcomes as needed since the Student Learning Assessment Plan is built around measuring these outcomes. The outcomes need to be as clear as possible and applicable to all users of the plan. Working with a team and gathering feedback throughout the process is beneficial for building a strong foundation of assessment practices.

Data Policies

The data policies section of the initial plan needed more detail. The creator of the initial plan did not receive any data with the submitted reports from library instructors, mostly due to unclear definitions and policies. The data policies section of the initial plan did not provide the support users needed, and the revised plan tried to fix this.

In the new iteration of the plan, work was done to ensure that data policies were clear and provided more directions to each section. This portion includes sections about gathering data, securing and storing data, accessing data, reporting data, and using data.

The gathering data section was expanded to include protocols on encrypting data with identifiable information and the recommendation not to collect identifiable information if it is unnecessary. There were also training sessions that covered all aspects of the data gathering section in detail. The student success and inclusion librarian also met with individual subject teams to discuss these data policies. Most questions during these meetings were about gathering data and what qualifies as data.

There are also sections about reporting data, retaining data, and using data. The new approach to this part of the Student Learning Assessment Plan was to give users the ability to learn about the differences in data collected and provide expectations for data use. An appendix was also added that detailed how to encrypt and share data with identifiable student information.

Data policies can be difficult to convey to library instructors. We recommend you look through your university's website for data policy recommendations and incorporate those into your plan.

Additional Assessment Tools

During the initial plan and review period, it became clear that more support for assessing student learning was needed to give library instructors the tools to be successful in their assessment efforts. In the survey about the plan, library instructors asked for more examples of assessment projects and support in creating assessment projects for upper-level undergraduate courses and graduate courses. In answer to these needs, we created a student learning assessment toolkit and a library curriculum map. We also implemented training about student learning assessment throughout each year. Finally, we developed a rubric for internal use, to assess reports that library instructors submit, so that training can be created for the next year to meet the needs of the plan's users. Each of these documents and new practices are rooted in supporting library instructors and improving the assessment practices of the University Libraries, which will ultimately improve the information literacy instruction.

Student Learning Assessment Toolkit

The Student Learning Assessment Toolkit includes sample assessment ideas that library instructors can use to measure student learning with the Student Learning Assessment Plan. Each idea is tied directly to a learning outcome outlined in the plan, so that instructors can view this toolkit at the beginning of each assessment cycle to gather ideas. Library instructors are not required to use these ideas and may edit or change them in any capacity to fit the needs of their classes. The toolkit also clearly states that these ideas are not the only ways to assess student learning in a classroom but are a starting point. It was important to offer a training session dedicated to explaining the different projects in the toolkit as well.

In the creation of this toolkit, a large group of library instructors from the Teaching and Learning Team brainstormed possible assessment projects. There was an emphasis on providing suggestions for library instructors that are new to assessment or want to refresh their assessment practices. The group also focused on projects that would be attainable with varying levels of course faculty support and buy-in and can be achieved in a one-shot library session. Ideas for how to assess standard lessons and activities that are used in library instruction at Mason and how they fit within the Student Learning Assessment Plan were also included.

Having an assessment toolkit to point to when people ask for ideas of assessment projects is a good instrument to build as you write your student learning assessment plan. Creating the toolkit also helped to contextualize and think through what the student learning outcomes meant and tighten up any language that was not clear in the initial round of revisions. It was also helpful to include several different library instructors with varying levels of student learning assessment experience to make sure there is a diversity of project ideas.

Curriculum Map

The Library Curriculum Map was created as a guide to how to use the learning outcomes from the Student Learning Assessment Plan in different levels of courses. The curriculum map introduces four levels of knowledge at which to teach our standardized learning outcomes: Introduced, Reinforced, Emphasized, and Mastered.

- Introduced: This is the first time a student will be hearing about this concept at the college level.
- Reinforced: A student is expected to have heard about this concept before coming to this course, but a student at this level is still focused on understanding/comprehending the concept being taught. Students begin application of this concept in this course.
- Emphasized: A student is expected to have tested this concept out before but is learning more complex issues about the concept in this course.
- Mastered: A student has a grasp of the complex issues surrounding this topic and pushes beyond these issues to trying to solve them.

The learning outcomes are mapped to instruction levels the University Libraries teach to show what level of information literacy knowledge should be expected of students and taught by instructors. It also emphasizes throughout the document that every learning outcome is not expected to be taught in all classes and that each class should be customized for the needs of the students.

In order to assist library instructors in creating sub-outcomes that match the level of instruction, examples of sub-outcomes that could be used in instruction settings were developed (see Table 7.1).

The curriculum map also aligns with university policies regarding reporting assessment efforts since academic departments are required to have curriculum maps in their assessment reporting structures.

Ultimately, the process of creating a curriculum map led to further discussions and clarifications of the learning outcomes and teaching strategies at our institution. The goal of this curriculum map is to give library instructors a way to think through their instructional learning outcomes and how they change according to different levels of instruction. It is recommended to think through the process of creating a curriculum map thoughtfully, as this was a time-consuming process.

TABLE 7.1 Example learning outcomes, corresponding to ascending levels of topic mastery

Criteria	Introduced	Reinforced	Emphasized	Mastered
Students identify a research question to begin their search process.	Students describe the qualities of a research question.	Students apply the qualities of a research question to their unique project.	Students revise their own research questions based on their research findings.	Students critique their research questions for adherence to disciplinary best practices.

Creating a Community of Practice

In addition to creating supportive documents for library instructors to refer to when building assessment tools, more trainings about student learning assessment and a community of practice around student learning assessment were created.

The Student Learning Assessment Community of Practice coordinates discussions and professional development opportunities for student learning assessment. This group works to identify barriers to assessment of student learning and provide trainings on these obstacles to library instructors. The intention of offering an ongoing community is to continually keep student learning assessment at the forefront of library instruction discussions, give library instructors a venue to ask questions about assessment, and give the community a space to learn from each other.

It is important to offer multiple formats, as every library instructor has different skill levels with student learning assessment. Offering training meetings, interactive workshops, and group working time ensures that every library instructor has an opportunity to have their personal needs met. Creating a community around student learning assessment has allowed library instructors to learn from each other about assessment practices and receive feedback on their projects throughout the year.

Evaluation of Assessment Reports

Another change to the assessment process is to implement an evaluation of assessment reports that library instructors submit each year. We created a rubric to aid in this process, with the goal to use this evaluation to inform the trainings needed for the next academic year, not to punish library instructors for their struggles. Library instructors will also be surveyed about how they used the supporting documentation to help us continuously improve these resources and anchor them in library instructor use.

Conclusion

The Student Learning Assessment Plan was not only a guide for assessment practices in information literacy, but it was a tool to foster a culture of instructional assessment in the University Libraries. To that end, the plan was successful. Upon reflection on the process of developing, implementing, and revising the plan, we recognized the need for more training, communication, and support for library instructors throughout the assessment cycle. The three-year timeline and cycle of the Student Learning Assessment Plan enabled this type of reflection and revision.

Setbacks to the assessment process have occurred and undoubtedly will continue as the University Libraries grows and develops as an organization. As the second iteration of the Student Learning Assessment Plan began, all library instruction at Mason transitioned to online learning due to COVID-19. Assessing fully online learning brings with it unique challenges and opportunities. While assessment processes are different, in many ways data collection is easier; however, with this comes a need for greater vigilance and attention to student privacy concerns. Additional setbacks are anticipated, but the systemic approach to student learning assessment will hopefully help mitigate them. The emphasis for the Student Learning Assessment Plan will continue to be improvement of student learning and library instruction. As new library instructors join the University Libraries our improved trainings and support aims to ease the learning curve for student learning assessment.

When undertaking building or revising a Student Learning Assessment Plan, there are several key takeaways from the project at Mason that can help you build a robust assessment plan. It is important to be responsive to institutional goals and priorities and incorporate them in your plan. Communication with stakeholders is vital at all stages of building and guiding your plan to ensure compliance with the plan's goals and understanding among library instructors. Navigating an instructional assessment space can be difficult, so providing trainings and support for library instructors throughout the life cycle of the plan is essential to keeping your plan on track. Each institution's plans will be slightly different, as assessment plans should be built where your institution is with student learning assessment and highlight your institution's resources for assessment practices.

The Student Learning Assessment Plan is not without its flaws – both in its implementation and its function within the University Libraries. As practitioners dedicated to improving our instructional practices, we must also work to improve documents like the Student Learning Assessment Plan in order to best serve the learning needs of our students.

References

American Library Association. (2012). *Assessment in Action: Academic libraries and student success*. http://www.ala.org/acrl/AiA

Bowles-Terry, M., Millet, M., & Travis, T.A. (2015). "Final assignment: A draft assessment plan" in ACRL Immersion Program. *Assessment Immersion Program participant notebook*. Association of College & Research Libraries.

Commission on Colleges of the Southern Association of Colleges and Schools. (2012). *Principles of accreditation: Foundations for quality enhancement*. https://sacscoc.org/app/uploads/2019/08/2012PrinciplesOfAccreditation1st.pdf.

George Mason Students as Scholars Initiative. (2016). *Students as scholars program rubric*. George Mason University. https://oscar.gmu.edu/wp-content/uploads/Students-as-Scholars-Program-Rubric-September-2016-1.pdf

George Mason University Libraries. (n.d.). *Student learning assessment plan*. Retrieved June 12, 2021, from https://library.gmu.edu/learning/assessment.

George Mason University. (2013). *George Mason University: 2014-2024 strategic plan*. George Mason University.

George Mason University. (2014). *Development of critical thinking rubric*. http://masoncore.gmu.edu/wp-content/uploads/2021/09/Critical-Thinking-Rubric-GMU.pdf

Kirker, M.J. (2016). *One-minute papers: Acclimating librarians to student learning assessment in library instruction* [Poster presentation]. Library Assessment Conference, Arlington, VA.

Kirker, M.J., Oberlies, M., Hernandez, C., & DeWaay, S. (2021). Teaching squares: Improving instruction through observation and self-reflection. *College & Research Libraries News, 82*(8), 370–373. 10.5860/crln.82.8.370

Oakleaf, M. (2009). The information literacy instruction assessment cycle: A guide for increasing student learning and improving librarian instructional skills. *Journal of Documentation, 65*(4), 539–560. 10.1108/00220410910970249

Oakleaf, M. (2010). Writing information literacy assessment plans: A guide to best practice. *Communications in Information Literacy, 3*(2), 80–90. 10.15760/comminfolit.2010.3.2.73

PART V
Leading Change

8

THAT'S NOT THE WAY WE'VE ALWAYS DONE IT: COORDINATING RESEARCH INSTRUCTION WITH INNOVATION, TEAMWORK, ASSESSMENT, AND COLLABORATION

Emily Z. Brown and Susan Souza-Mort

Introduction

Working at a community college is both a rewarding and challenging experience. We have greater access to students because of the smaller size of the student body compared to a larger four-year institution. However, because of open enrollment policies, we also deal with students with a wide variety of skills. Our programming is aimed at making every student, at every academic level, successful.

We are writing this chapter as a partnership, which is how we have approached much of our work at the college. We both work at Bristol Community College, located across five locations in southeastern Massachusetts. Emily Brown, a graduate of the University of Pittsburgh, joined Bristol Community College in 2013 as Coordinator of Library Research and Instruction based in Fall River. Emily had worked previously at higher education institutions in Oklahoma (two universities and a law school). Susan Souza-Mort is a graduate of Simmons University SLIS in Boston and worked at Baker Library, Harvard. In 2002, she went back to her roots, to where her education began, at Bristol Community College, where she now coordinates library services for the New Bedford campus. We both have a strong affinity for teaching and collaboration, and a love for learning.

Occasionally, at conferences, we have heard concerns about the academic rigor of a community college information literacy education. In actuality, community college librarians work consistently and creatively to introduce information literacy concepts across the curriculum. In fact, our work at our institution has resulted in information literacy being a required core competency to a Bristol Community College education. We work closely with faculty to ensure students understand the multifaceted adventure that is research.

DOI: 10.4324/9781003038634-14

Though community colleges face many challenges (among them a lack of a robust budget, enrollment rollercoasters, and a diverse student body in age, background, and ability), we have argued that the atmosphere of a community college aids all levels of academic pursuit, and we believe that community college librarians are uniquely positioned to have an outsized impact on our students due to the close personal relationships we build with them and their faculty (Brown & Souza-Mort, 2017).

We have also experienced a large amount of institutional change since 2018. Our library merged with the Learning Commons and all our spaces were renovated and updated. Two of our campus locations moved entirely. This upheaval created several issues regarding morale. We have also experienced a revolving door of leadership (and the leadership styles that come with it). We lost several staff members during the pandemic to lay-offs and are facing our third reorganization in four years as of April 2022.

This chapter will discuss how we (in collaboration with our colleagues) harnessed this incredible flux to grow our instruction program and extend campus-wide influence despite the roadblocks and challenges we have encountered.

The Catalyst for Change

Prior to the start of our partnership in 2013, information literacy sessions at Bristol Community College were hands-off and lecture based. In addition, teaching was not assessed, and faculty relationships were not collaborative; in fact, faculty members were rarely present for library classes. Our previous coordinator had just retired, and the atmosphere was ripe for innovation and a new approach to information literacy. We immediately realized that between us we had a lot of bold ideas and an opportunity to try something new.

A cohesive team is crucial for any experiment in instruction to flourish. The partnership we created was a solid base from which we could encourage participation in new ideas and innovative efforts from each librarian. We encouraged our team to try new things and adapted our instruction as each member discovered new ways to teach.

We began our work together during the winter of 2013 and 2014 assessing the one-shot. At the time we taught instruction as most librarians do: during single sessions in the classroom. We focused on basic searching skills, common information literacy strategies, and traditional and digital material. While this met the basic needs of the students, we wondered if we could develop strategies to have a greater impact on student learning.

At this point, the College began a year-long college-wide assessment effort using the American Association of Colleges and Universities (AAC&U) (2013) Valid Assessment of Learning in Undergraduate Education (VALUE) Rubrics and we jumped at a chance to assess our instruction program. We wanted to concentrate on finding evidence of the incorporation of information literacy techniques in written student artifacts after participation in one-shot instruction sessions. The Information Literacy VALUE Rubric was critical in our assessment as well as in later efforts to create a rubric of our own.

We began by gathering a small group of faculty to assess their students' work. These volunteers represented the departments of English, Early Childhood Education, and Clinical Lab Science. After we read each artifact, we normed them against the rubric to come to a common score. What we found was not surprising—students who attend only traditional one-shot sessions do not master the skills that enable them to meet the higher benchmarks of the VALUE rubric (Brown et al., 2014). Specifically, students had challenges with synthesizing information, assessment of sources, and with citing sources and understanding when to paraphrase.

These findings forced us to think about how we might approach this critical gap in learning. What resulted from this initial report was a multi-faceted approach to student learning that incorporated multiple research sessions, assessment, student research appointments, a for-credit information literacy course, embedded librarian programs, and closer collaboration with the Writing Center and faculty.

Introducing Chasers and Multi-sessions

We proposed that faculty act upon our conclusions and incorporate information literacy concepts more rigorously into their research assignments and across the entire semester (Brown et al, 2014). We encouraged faculty to think about information literacy as a multi-tiered system that is infused into every level of academic work; incorporating information literacy throughout the semester would bolster their students' understanding of themselves within the information environment.

We made deep programmatic changes to our information literacy offerings, moving away from one-shots when possible and incorporating multiple sessions into a single course when practical. The new model focused on giving faculty the opportunity to choose how we (the librarians) interacted with their students. They could continue to choose one-shots, they could have a one shot with a short 20-minute chaser session on another date, or they could do two or more full information literacy sessions (or, as we call them, multi-sessions).

Faculty were immediately interested in this idea of revolutionizing our instruction program. Over the following semester, we had a total of 85 faculty members try our new model of information literacy. Out of a total of 192 sessions, 130 were traditional one-shots, 26 were multiple sessions, and 24 were one-shots with a chaser (Brown & Souza-Mort, 2015, pp. 406). We were able to develop strong partnerships with several faculty who have worked with us every semester since to incorporate information literacy across the semester.

We realized that chaser sessions, while funny as a gimmick, were not really doing what we had hoped. Our research showed that multi-sessions were much more successful in teaching students the skills they needed to incorporate information literacy skills into their papers and beyond (Brown & Souza-Mort, 2015).

Transforming the Framework into a Rubric

The publication of the Association for College & Research Libraries (ACRL's) *Framework for Information Literacy for Higher Education* (The Framework) (2016) coincided with our efforts to track the impact of both our one-shot instruction sessions and multi-session classes. While we found AAC&U's VALUE rubric sufficient, the Framework offered us a more in-depth description of what skills we were hoping to teach our students. The Framework allowed us to visualize specific student learning outcomes (SLOs) and apply them to our pedagogy.

Inspired by our VALUE rubric experience, we began to develop a rubric using the Framework competencies. In doing so, we realized, based on the expected proficiency levels, that the Framework skills were aimed at a four-year college experience rather than a two-year experience. For example, the "capstone" skills are likely more relevant to advanced, graduate-level learners. We worked with Bristol faculty to improve the rubric and tailor it to the needs of two-year students. In workshops with faculty and colleagues we simplified language for non-librarian consumption, we chose which competencies could be fulfilled by two-year students and applied them to student artifacts (see Table 8.1). We found that this new rubric fits our assessment needs and began to apply it in our regular norming sessions and the college adopted our rubric for college-wide assessment.

Collaboration for Innovation

Coordinating a library research and instruction program can be challenging, but having a confidant and co-conspirator can help to introduce new ideas to the team. Additionally, this allowed us to collaborate on ideas, solicit feedback from one another, and ultimately enhance instructional offerings. Luckily, our department embraces the ideas of five independent, creative, and innovative librarians who have been willing to try new approaches, with no assurance that they would succeed. Over the years, we have developed a close partnership within the department, which supports and emboldens one another to innovate and experiment. For us, our failures have been just as important as our successes.

Each librarian on our staff represents a unique campus community which allows us to develop deep and collaborative relationships with the faculty at each Bristol location. These relationships have allowed for specific in-depth instruction opportunities to develop.

As the librarian for the New Bedford campus, Susan was able to directly interact with faculty, by dropping into their classrooms at the end of their classes. New Bedford's small campus environment, located in an urban historical downtown setting in an old 19th-century building, made it easy to stop by and make an introduction. As a result, Susan's developed close ties to the faculty, especially adjuncts who typically leave right after their classes to drive to another campus.

As the coordinator of research and instruction, Emily needed to establish relationships with faculty on all campuses, but primarily in Fall River, the largest of

TABLE 8.1 Bristol Community College Assessment Rubric

001ﾃ

	Capstone	Milestones		Benchmark
	3	2	1	0
Authority is Constructed and Contextual	• Sources are authoritative (via scholarship, societal position, or primary experience) • Incorporates informed skepticism of authoritative claims. • Identifies sources that may challenge the authority, acknowledges biases.	• Sources are mostly authoritative, some sources of questionable authority are quoted. • Begins to challenge the authority of sources presented, acknowledges biases. • Begins to incorporate informed skepticism of authoritative claims.	• Most sources are not authoritative, though a few credible sources are consulted. • Does not fully challenge the authority of sources presented, does not acknowledge biases. • Does not incorporate informed skepticism of authoritative claims.	• All sources are not authoritative. • Does not challenge the authority of sources presented, does not acknowledge biases. • Does not incorporate informed skepticism of authoritative claims.
Information has Value	• Identifies individuals or groups of individuals that are underrepresented. • Identifies competing influences, interests, agendas, or bias. • References are fully documented, with no error.	• Research is fully documented, with errors. • Begins to understand marginalized groups within the systems that produce and disseminate information. • Begins to formulate and apply original research.	• Research is not fully documented. • Does not fully grasp why marginalized groups within the systems that produce and disseminate information. • Incorporates original ideas, does not conduct original research. does not conduct original research.	• Research is not documented. • Does not understand why some marginalized groups within the systems that produce and disseminate information. • Does not incorporate original ideas or research.

(Continued)

TABLE 8.1 (Continued)

	Capstone	Milestones	Milestones	Benchmark
	3	2	1	0
Research as Inquiry	• Determines the appropriate scope of investigation, is able to narrow the topic. • Seeks multiple perspectives. • Draws reasonable conclusions based on analysis and interpretation of information.	• Begins to identify areas that require further research. • Begins to limit the scope of investigation. • Draws several reasonable conclusions based on analysis and interpretation of information.	• Areas that require further research are only briefly addressed. • Does not appropriately limit the scope of investigation, proposes questions that are not answered. • Begins to draw reasonable conclusions based on analysis and interpretation of information.	• Areas that require further research are not addressed. • Does not limit the scope of investigation. • Draws unreasonable conclusions based on misinterpretation of information.
Scholarship as Conversation	• Fully summaries the changes in scholarly perspective over time. • Identifies the impact of a particular source or idea on the topic. • Identifies areas where more research is required.	• Begins to incorporate the evolving discourse of a topic, partially summarizing the changes is scholarly perspective over time. • Begins to identify the impact a particular source makes to the disciplinary knowledge.	• Addresses a few aspects of the discourse of a topic. • Does not fully explain the impact a particular source makes to the disciplinary knowledge.	• Does not address the scholarly discourse of a topic. • Does not explain the impact a particular source makes to the disciplinary knowledge.

Searching is Strategic Exploration			
• Identifies the appropriate source for the information needed. • Addresses multiple aspects of a topic. • Acquires an appropriate number of sources required to fulfill the information need.	• Identifies several interested parties who might produce information about the topic accesses that information. • Begins to address multiple aspects of a topic, covering avenues that arise during the research process. • Acquires a few more sources than what are required to fulfill the information need.	• Identifies a single interested party who might produce information about the topic accesses that information. • Addresses a few aspects of a topic. • Acquires exactly the number of sources required to fulfill the information need.	• Does not identify interested parties who might produce information on the topic. • Addresses only one aspect of a topic. • Does not acquire the number of sources required to fulfill the information need.

Source: Adapted from the ACRL *Framework for Information Literacy.*

the four physical Bristol Community College locations. Our organizational structure allows for each librarian to have a home campus at which to develop and maintain relationships with faculty. Often, if one of us works with a faculty member on one campus, then that faculty member will work with another one of us on another campus.

These close relationships have helped us to create several unique classes in partnership with faculty. These unique multi-sessions have covered everything from synthesizing sources to infographics and the re-investigation of a century-old murder. These instructors bring their students multiple times into the library or invite the librarian to their classroom, allowing us to create close relationships with their students as well. Students will often then find "their librarian" and will stick with us for research appointments for all their classes until they graduate. These multi-sessions have led to students booking research appointments with us weekly over the entire semester.

Each librarian on every Bristol Community College campus has developed new and creative strategies for teaching (see Appendix 1). We meet monthly and exchange ideas, often adopting one another's methods for instruction. This has made our instruction program truly nimble and adaptive.

Moving Outside the Classroom

At each of our campus locations our team began to adopt instruction strategies and provide workshops that went far beyond traditional information literacy based on in-class research assignments. This approach allowed us to lay the groundwork for a stronger role for information literacy in the college culture. We began to engage the college in discourse on current events and social issues which attracted students, faculty, staff, and the general public.

The college-wide support for these efforts ultimately opened the door for us to address important information literacy issues such as voting rights, misinformation campaigns, and Holocaust and Genocide education.

Voting Rights

Librarians are often vital sources of information for the public when we go to the polls. During the 2016 and 2018 election cycles there was a campus-wide effort to encourage our students, faculty, and staff to vote. We partnered with Civic Engagement to offer *Bayhawks Vote* workshops, host registration drives, and give in-class presentations on the importance of voting.

We also partnered with the Women's Center to present these themes to the local community, including state legislators. The College then incorporated our presentations into their "Pizza and Politics" program, which allowed us further access to students.

Misinformation/Meme Workshops

With the 2016 elections approaching and the onslaught of "fake news," Bristol librarians were swift to respond with interactive workshops utilizing memes to help students learn how to fact check using reputable sources. In New Bedford, Susan started with a survey prior to the class modeled after Dr. Allison Head's "How Students Engage with News: Five Takeaways for Educators, Journalists, and Librarians" (2018). The results resembled Dr. Head's findings that students received their news from Facebook, Snapchat, and YouTube. By passing out memes to students that covered liberal and conservative biases, they were taught how to fact check using reputable sites such as PolitiFact (https://www.politifact. com) to verify the meme's information. This hands-on approach was well received by students and faculty alike, and all campus locations adopted it. Ultimately, this lesson plan morphed into a concentrated view of mis/disinformation during Trump's presidency with an eventual focus on self-radicalization (Brown & Souza-Mort, 2021).

Thanks to the strong personal relationships librarians had developed with faculty on their campuses, the misinformation workshops were often tailored to specific classes. In Fall River, we focused on the political intrigue happening through interference from Russia and misinformation that led to incidents like the Comet Pizzeria incident (United States Attorney's Office, 2017). In Attleboro, Laura Hogan developed a class focused solely on medical misinformation for a professor in health sciences. Considering the pandemic, this was a prophetic choice of instructional topic.

College-Wide Colloquia

In 2019, the world witnessed two major acts of hate-based terror: the Christchurch Mosque shootings and the massacre at the Tree of Life Synagogue (Roose, 2019). Our colleagues in the English department, Farah Habib and Denise DiMarzio, decided that we must act as a college community to condemn hatred, bigotry, and acts of violence. They created a year-long colloquium entitled *A More Perfect Union: Bristol Stands Against Hate.*

This colloquium brought together academics from all departments on campus. For example, the Theatre faculty staged a play on microaggressions, and we were invited to present research on how to combat misinformation. We were able to focus on more than traditional political misinformation, but also on Russian misinformation in both Ukraine and the United States, paving the way for later information sessions on Ukraine.

Our presentation also gave us an opportunity to explore how national and international right-wing groups use memes to radicalize young people who find them on the internet via searching and social media. These presentations were held in such a way so that faculty could bring their classes and the public could attend. After one of our sessions, we were invited to present our misinformation session at the local public library. Unfortunately, the COVID-19 pandemic delayed this partnership until restrictions began to ease.

After the events on January 6, 2021, we approached our colleagues in the English Department hoping to update our presentation on self-radicalization. They were unable to commit to a second colloquium but offered us the opportunity to take over: so, we did. We felt that it was perfect timing to focus specifically on not only self-radicalization, but on COVID-19 misinformation as well.

In the spring of 2021, we began to plan the colloquium entitled *A More Perfect Union: Diffusing Disinformation and Promoting Critical Thought* to start that fall. We invited investigative journalist Mike Beaudet from Boston's WCVB to discuss the importance of journalism to a participatory democracy for our Fall Keynote. Dr. Mónica Feliú-Mójer, a scientist and science communicator, discussed the importance of truth in science as our Spring Keynote. We then invited Bristol Community College professors Steve Frechette, Robyn Worthington, Ron Weisberger, Mary Rapien, and librarian Laura Hogan who discussed how the FBI is tracking the insurrectionists, misinformation in history, science and misinformation, and medical misinformation respectively. We also partnered with the Multicultural Center and Director Rob Delaleu to cohost a session on "uncomfortable conversations."

We presented "Do Your Research," on self-radicalization, in November of 2021 and rekindled our partnership with the local public library to give our presentation there as well (Bowles, 2021). We hope to partner with the local public libraries more as we continue to provide workshops that are important to civic engagement and participation.

These collaborative presentations have helped to raise our profile across the college and have increased our visibility to our colleagues on the faculty and in other centers on campus. We have been able to make information literacy relatable across disciplines by partnering with diverse departments.

Ukraine Teach-In

In the spring of 2022 as Vladimir Putin and the Russian armed forces amassed along Ukraine's border, the associate dean of the library wanted to host a discussion about the events. We held a hybrid (in person/online) event to answer questions and talk about the history involved. We invited two history professors, Rebecca Benya-Soderbom and Eddie Guimont, who joined Emily in speaking. Then, after Russia invaded the sovereign state of Ukraine, we held four separate 'teach-ins.' These sessions were informal and in-person only. We pulled chairs into a circle and talked about current events. These teach-ins attracted faculty, staff, students, and administrators and gave the college an outlet to discuss what was happening.

The Poisoned Path Workshops

In a critical on-campus partnership, Emily worked with Dr. Ron Weisberger, the director of the Bristol Community College Holocaust and Genocide Center, to create a collection of digital and print material focused on genocide. This collection inspired The Poisoned Path Project, which focuses on encouraging community college faculty to teach about genocide, no matter their discipline (https://libguides.bristolcc.edu/Poisoned_Path).

The collection was opened officially in March of 2022, with several state legislators, the Ambassador from Israel to New England Meron Reuben, and son of Holocaust survivor Paul Truer invited as speakers (Cooney, 2022). This collection is one-of-a-kind in southern Massachusetts.

As of the writing of this chapter, we are planning several workshops that will make use of The Poisoned Path Project. Faculty from all over the college are invited to attend and can receive a stipend to incorporate the topic of genocide into their classes. The first offering filled up in one day, and we are looking for funding opportunities to offer a second session, for which there is already a waiting list.

Learning Communities

Bristol Community College has recently embraced the high-impact practice of learning communities (AAC&U, 2022). This coincided with our development of an information literacy course. We have submitted a course proposal to the curriculum committee of the college that entails joining a semester-long research-based information literacy course with a research-heavy class like Sociology. A colleague from the Sociology Department has agreed to test this class with us pending its approval.

The class will embed information literacy skills in our "College Success Central" classes (another high impact practice). Our class will teach one credit of college-ready skills and two credits of information literacy, all tied to the course in the learning community (sociology). The sociology course includes a scaffolded semester-long research assignment, which we would focus on as the research project in the information literacy half of the learning community.

Lessons and Conclusion

We are coming together now, post-pandemic, with a new focus and drive. New leadership has combined our services to create an inescapable net of support for students in both research and tutoring assistance. This new focus is allowing opportunities for collaboration and discovery as we merge services and blend pedagogy.

We have emerged from stressful years of near-constant change, crises, and pandemic. We have begun the work of bringing students back to campus and have transitioned back to our offices. We have been a team long enough to know each other's strengths and weaknesses. This deep inter-departmental knowledge has allowed us to really engage students and faculty with information literacy theory and practice.

We have learned many lessons over the years of working closely together, the most important of which is to not be afraid to try new things. You will fail. We can promise you that. Failures can provide an opportunity for innovation and redesign that work out even better. Strong and trusting relationships with faculty are also helpful in experimenting in the classroom. Often, when our faculty colleagues feel they are a part of our experiments, they are more excited to try new modes of instruction. Bring faculty into your planning process—their knowledge of the assignment and your knowledge of information literacy can together create something transformational in the classroom.

Partnerships with faculty are important, but so are relationships with other staff departments like tutoring and the writing center. These relationships can help to create something amazing and trailblazing, even if you haven't been consolidated into a "Learning Commons." We were told years ago that the Writing Center on campus was mimicking our instructional model because we have been so successful in engaging faculty in our work. When a faculty member requests instruction, they can request support from tutoring and the Writing Center on the same form. We have created co-workshops with the Writing Center focused on citation skills. These partnerships help to solidify the idea of support services into the minds of students as they navigate their academic careers.

Some ideas may sound crazy (the best ideas usually are); do not be afraid to try them. Many of our successful information literacy classes were born out of brainstorming sessions. In other words, turn the "that's not how we've always done it" into "that's how we could do it."

Assessment is crucial. Involve faculty in your efforts to evaluate your effectiveness in the classroom. This can be an opportunity to talk about assignment design and hands-on learning. Utilize student artifacts and employ rubrics. Schedule regular norming sessions that will help you gauge what is working and what needs to be adjusted.

Employ student surveys after each information literacy class to help gauge students' understanding of the lesson, and what they retained during your session. This will also be useful in fine tuning your lesson plans to make them more engaging and efficient.

We have had opportunities to build something new and are moving into a brand-new phase as a Library Learning Commons. The pandemic has made a dent in our enrollment, but as we work to create new partnerships, we know that our past efforts have left us well positioned to conduct outreach to students and faculty as we return to campus. We will continue to focus on learning from each other, trying new things and creating a mindset that is open and adventurous. We aren't afraid of failure, and we refuse to say, "that's the way we've always done it."

References

References

A more perfect union: Diffusing misinformation and promoting critical thought. (2021). Bristol Community College. https://www.bristolcc.edu//bristolcommunity/facultystaff/bristolcolloquiumseries/diffusingdisinformation/

Association of American Colleges & Universities. (2013). *VALUE rubrics*. AAC&U. https://www.aacu.org/value/rubrics/information-literacy

Association of American Colleges & Universities. (2022). *High impact practices*. AAC&U. https://www.aacu.org/trending-topics/high-impact

Association of College and Research Libraries. (2016). *Framework for information literacy for higher education*. ACRL. https://www.ala.org/acrl/standards/ilframework

Bowles, S.Q. (2021). *Don't get reeled in by fake news, speakers tell audience*. Dartmouth Week. https://dartmouth.theweektoday.com/article/don%E2%80%99t-get-reeled-fake-news-speakers-tell-audience/55227

Brown, E., & Souza-Mort, S. (2021, September 20). *Hello? Hello? Are you stuck in an echo chamber? Managing and identifying misinformation in the era of Trump* [Conference presentation]. European Conference on Information Literacy, online. http://ecil2021.ilconf.org/wp-content/uploads/sites/9/2021/12/ECIL2021BoA-final-2nd-ed.pdf

Brown, E., & Souza-Mort, S. (2017, September 18–21). *Leading together: Harnessing the community college atmosphere to impact student learning* [Conference presentation]. European Conference on Information Literacy, St. Malo, Brittany, France. http://ecil2017.ilconf.org/

Brown, E., & Souza-Mort, S. (2015, March 25). LEAP rubrics and information literacy assessment: We think you need a chaser with that one-shot [Paper presentation]. In *ACRL 2015 Conference Proceedings*. ACRL 2015: Creating Sustainable Community, Portland, OR (403–408). ACRL.

Brown, E., Souza-Mort, S., Grandchamp, J., Norberg, C., Richter, L., & St. George, D. (2014). *Report from the LEAP rubric assessment project at the Bristol Community College Libraries*. Bristol Community College. https://libguides.bristolcc.edu/ld.php?content_id=15803741

Cooney, A. (2022). *Bristol Community College's new library collection focuses on the Holocaust and genocide*. Herald News. https://www.heraldnews.com/story/news/2022/03/25/new-genocide-library-collection-bristol-community-college/7153343001/

Head, A., Whiby, J., Metaxas, P.T., Macmillan, M., & Cohen, D. (2018). "How students engage with news: Five takeaways for educators, journalists, and librarians." Project Information Literacy Research Institute, https://projectinfolit.org/publications/news-study/

Roose, K. (2019). *A mass murder of, and for, the internet*. New York Times. https://www.nytimes.com/2019/03/15/technology/facebook-youtube-christchurch-shooting.html

United States Attorney's Office. (2017). *North Carolina man sentenced to four-year prison term for armed assault at northwest Washington pizza restaurant*. US Department of Justice. https://www.justice.gov/usao-dc/pr/north-carolina-man-sentenced-four-year-prison-term-armed-assault-northwest-washington

9

TIME FOR A REBOOT! MAKING SPACE FOR INSTRUCTION PROGRAM DEVELOPMENT

Anne C. Behler

Introduction

One thing instruction librarians have in common is the need to be responsive to paradigm shifts within our field, within higher education, as well as in our own institutions. The transition from the *Information Literacy Competency Standards for Higher Education* (the *Standards*) to the *ACRL Framework for Information Literacy in Higher Education* (the *Framework*) was one such shift that affected us all (Association for College & Research Libraries [ACRL], 2000; ACRL, 2015). More recently, we have faced the challenges of teaching modality changes, necessitated by the COVID-19 pandemic. Evolutions such as these call on instruction librarians to be nimble, and instruction coordinators must lead the way. This can feel like a tall order, when instruction programs are ever active, librarians always teaching, faculty members and curricular partners faithfully requesting library integrations.

Library instruction is a labor of love for many, and a source of an incredible amount of work. We regularly live the ebbs and flows of our students' work – papers, speeches, and citation problems. There are times in the semester when we teach so many classes it feels we can't come up for air. Thus, it can be a great challenge to also assess, innovate, create, and try new things. Yet, we all endeavor to improve our practice because ultimately what we strive for is information literacy instruction that is intentional, relevant, and meaningful.

Given the seemingly constant demands on an instruction librarian's time, how can we truly take stock of our programs? The possibility I offer in this chapter is to stop. Stop teaching. As the instruction coordinator, make the space for you and your colleagues to think, to reimagine what is possible, and to gather a collective breath of reenergizing air. During 2018 and 2019, we did just that as the Penn State University Libraries, Library Learning Services (LLS) Department. We stopped teaching for ENGL 15, Penn State's first-year rhetoric and composition

DOI: 10.4324/9781003038634-15

class, for the entirety of Spring, 2019. During this time, we undertook to align our teaching activities with our stated objectives, inventory the many instructional activities and modes we employ, and take stock of our areas of expertise. In so doing, we would carry forward with an instruction program that makes meaningful differences for our students. Ultimately, the program 'Reboot' changed the way we approach foundational information literacy instruction, and we established habits of mind for regularly evaluating and evolving our teaching.

Background

Penn State is a large, land grant institution with nearly 90,000 students situated at 24 different campuses throughout the Commonwealth of Pennsylvania, as well as the online Penn State World Campus (Penn State Planning, Assessment, and Institutional Research, n.d.). All physical campuses include libraries, whose librarians primarily engage in teaching and research support for those locations. Approaches at each campus are unique and flexible to the population and courses being served; however, instruction librarians across Penn State continuously work toward a cohesive, coordinated instruction program. The Library Learning Services Department is situated at the University Park campus, and while this location is no longer referred to as the "main campus" of the university, it is the administrative hub for most university operations. Library Learning Services takes a strong leadership role in the development of teaching practices across the Commonwealth and collaborates with colleagues from other campuses to adapt teaching practices to those settings.

I joined Library Learning Services in 2006 as an information literacy librarian. At the time, the department comprised just five individuals and was at the beginning of a years-long expansion of both personnel and service. In 2012, I became the first officially titled instruction coordinator for the unit, assuming the responsibility of leading curriculum development, building instructional partnerships, and strategizing our pedagogical approaches to foundational information literacy instruction. Part of this strategy, as directed by our department head, was to evolve into a unit of specialized coordinators who could form an institutional hub of leadership in teaching and learning at the Penn State University Libraries. By 2018, Library Learning Services comprised twelve individuals: the Department Head, Instruction Coordinator, Student Engagement Coordinator, Outreach Coordinator, Online Learning Librarian, Learning Design Librarian, Learning Technologies Coordinator, OER librarian, three reference and instruction librarians, and one administrative support staff member. Except for the outreach coordinator and the administrative support staff member, all held faculty status. These individuals formed a departmental team, focused on leading foundational information literacy instruction, outreach and student engagement, as well as developing pedagogical practices and both physical and online learning environments. The department was also responsible for library instruction to several core university courses at the University Park campus, including English Rhetoric and Composition (ENGL 15), English as a Second Language: Composition for American Academic Communication II (ESL 15), Effective Speech (CAS 100), and a few other miscellaneous introductory classes. Additionally, instruction was offered to some courses and programs via a growing digital badges (micro-credentials) initiative, and the department led library orientation and outreach programming for thousands of students each year (Penn State University Libraries, 2021). In total, during the fall 2018 semester, LLS taught 131 individual one-shot instruction sessions for nearly 3,000 students, led a campus-wide annual orientation event for nearly 3,000 students, conducted outreach and orientation sessions for over 2,300 students, and held an end-of-semester "Destress Fest," attended by over 6,000 students (Library Learning Services, 2018). To say the least, the Learning Services plate was full, and the team members were feeling spread thin. We were not in a position that allowed for the strategically curated expertise to shine in meaningful ways – we were just too busy.

Finding Inspiration

If this were a film, I'd insert a record scratch sound effect here, and rewind the screen back to 2014. 2014 is the year that I attended the LOEX annual conference in Grand Rapids, Michigan. Sitting in a crowded hotel conference room and just two years into my role as instruction coordinator, I listened to Alan Carbery and Janet Cottrell (2014), then of Champlain College, deliver the session "Inquiry-based Learning Online: Designing and Delivering a Blended and Embedded Information Literacy Program." Carbery and Cottrell shared the story of a summer without library instruction – a summer during which their teaching unit could give complete focus to retooling their teaching for the undergraduates at Champlain. They, of course, went into detail about what specific changes they made to their program, why, and how; but what stuck with me was that they had *stopped teaching* in order to make *space* for it happen.

By 2018, it was clear that Library Learning Services could use a similar reset. We were incredibly busy – and by all counts incredibly successful – but we also needed desperately to come up for air. We needed *space*. Remembering the Champlain College librarians' approach to program revision, I approached the LLS department head with the idea that we, too, stop teaching for a semester so that we might assess our priorities, our current activities, and our goals, emerging with a strategic way forward for our program. With her support, I proposed the idea to the rest of the department, and together we made the decision to take our entire foundational library instruction program, apart from one-shots for ESL classes, offline for an entire semester. Cessation of face-to-face instruction for the ENGL 15 course, which accounted for 75% of the LLS teaching load, would buy an approximated 150 collaborative hours which had traditionally been used for preparatory and instructional time each semester. With this decision, the Library

Instruction Reboot was born. By the close of Summer, 2018, we had selected the Spring, 2019 semester to conduct our project.

Preparing to Make Space

Taking a library instruction program offline for a semester during the core academic year is no small task; however, we intentionally chose spring semester rather than summer so that we could fully engage our stakeholders in the process, and to make a symbolic statement about the importance of the Instruction Reboot. This would not *just* be a summer project; we would spend half of the full-operation academic term to immerse ourselves in the act of clearly defining our instructional program focus and priorities. It was important to us that we carefully plan how we would spend our chosen semester. Equally important was that we develop and carry out an open, mindful communication plan about the Reboot.

To get ourselves in the mindset for this endeavor, we began by reading *Essentialism: The Disciplined Pursuit of Less,* by Greg McKeown (2014), over the summer of 2018. While we did find some of McKeown's work to be problematic owing to the white, male, privileged point-of-view dominating, the book did provide some nuggets of wisdom, and our discussion of the work served as a catalyst to frame conversations about what our instruction program might look like if we were to center it on the practices that are most meaningful – those that will benefit and make the biggest difference for our students. When resources, including personnel, are finite, we must decide where best to apply those resources! Beginning in May 2018, LLS made use of several "mega meetings" – half-day, retreat-style meetings, held in person at a campus location outside the library – to define our goals and plans for the Library Instruction Reboot. As a unit, LLS established the following goals for Spring 2019:

- Emerge with an articulated teaching program.
- Define the scope for our curriculum.
- Develop new teaching activities for in-person, online, and hybrid scenarios.
- Identify curricular partners and goals/strategies for engaging with them.
- Plan for effective assessment of our teaching integrations.

During the Fall 2018 semester, between carrying out our typical instruction and outreach duties, we met frequently to develop a clear outline and structure for the Library Instruction Reboot. The common thread through these planning conversations was our desire to identify opportunities to provide *strategic* and *meaningful* learning opportunities, via whatever format made the most sense given the context. Through taking inventory of our expertise, instructional priorities, and articulated information literacy outcomes [see box 9.1], we identified three areas of focus for the Library Instruction Reboot and formed corresponding working teams.

BOX 9.1 FOUNDATIONAL LEARNING OBJECTIVES FOR LIBRARY INSTRUCTION

At the foundational level, students will be able to:

- recognize that there are a variety of resources available to assist in their research needs, including the Libraries' home page, the ENGL:015 or CAS:100 course guide, and the Ask a Librarian service.
- determine the most appropriate information source or search tool (e.g. LionSearch, Google, or other database) for their information need.
- distinguish between different information formats (scholarly article, newspaper article, blog, etc.) and determine the appropriate format for their research needs
- identify keywords based on their topics or research questions and revise their search terms as needed in order to conduct an effective search.
- use information resources in order to gain an understanding of a research topic and generate research questions.
- refine search results using built-in database features and/or search term refinement in order to locate resources that meet their specific information needs.
- critically evaluate different sources of information and identify key criteria needed in an authoritative source.

As they delve into the process of writing and research integration, students will be able to:

- locate citation generator tools and the libraries' citation guides in order to create accurate citations in the appropriate style.
- practice ethical use of information, avoiding plagiarism and copyright infringement, in order to produce academic-quality, original works.

Additionally, librarians strive to give students a strong sense of the library as a place for safe and supported academic activity.

The first, Foundational Learners, committed to study of our existing partnerships and teaching activities – including assessment – geared toward foundational information literacy learners. A primary target of study for this group was the ENGL 15: Rhetoric and Composition course. Housed within the Program in Writing and Rhetoric (PWR), the course represented the highest percentage of Library Learning Services' teaching portfolio. This group devised the following charge (Clossen, 2019):

- Assess the needs of our foundational user groups.
- Review the strengths and weaknesses of current and past approaches to foundational instruction.

- Complete an analysis of teaching models.
- Articulate a scaled way forward for foundational instruction.

As specific deliverables, the Foundational Learners sub-team would make a recommendation for how best to integrate library instruction into ENGL 15 and CAS 100 and provide evaluation of resource investment in teaching for foundational information literacy classes in all modes.

Distinctive Populations, as defined in the Association of Research Libraries (ARL) 2018 Research Library Impact Framework, was identified as a critical and emerging component of our teaching portfolio. Library Learning Services' robust student engagement and outreach efforts had already forged many successful partnerships with university entities supporting distinctive student populations such as veterans, first-generation college students, students of color, adult learners, and others. The Reboot afforded the opportunity for our second working team to examine these partnerships for possible curricular opportunities. The hope was to be able to dive deeper into information literacy instruction, thus supporting student success among populations who statistically have a more difficult road to attaining a college degree. In addition, the team would identify new opportunities for collaboration to explore (Amsberry, 2019).

Finally, even before 2020, web-based learning had become a rule, rather than an exception, for our students. One way that Library Learning Services had successfully met students in the online space was through a digital badge program. Since its inception in 2014, the digital badge program had grown exponentially. By fall 2018, it was clear that we needed to take time to discern an appropriate scale for the program, establish parameters around populations to target, identify colleagues to help lead and assess the program on an ongoing basis, create a team to evaluate student submissions, and identify strategies for future growth and assessment. Our third Reboot team, dedicated to addressing these issues and questions, planned a pilot using digital badges as an instructional delivery method for the resident ENGL 15 course to assess whether the model would be a viable one for that course. The Badges Team would also gather data – such as time spent evaluating responses – to make informed decisions about scale (Raish, 2019).

All Aboard: Enacting a Holistic Communication Plan

Communication about The Library Instruction Reboot was extremely complicated, and multi-faceted. The way we choose to talk about that which may seem unthinkable – even crazy – to our colleagues and academic partners is extraordinarily important. It was essential that we clearly articulate our plans and garner support among our stakeholders in library administration; our curricular partners, particularly those who would experience a change in their typical level of instruction; our outreach and engagement partners; and finally, but not least, our library colleagues.

Administration

The instruction coordinator at Penn State reports directly to the head of the Library Learning Services Department, who, in turn, reports directly to the associate dean with teaching and learning and undergraduate services in their portfolio. The individuals in these administrative roles in 2018 were both supportive of the Reboot, and that was largely because I was able to address several key points that may have caused them concern.

First, with the help of my colleagues in LLS, I was able to articulate a clear vision for the Reboot. The vision was that the entire department would be afforded the space of one academic semester to operate solely as a research and development unit for teaching and learning for foundational information literacy learners. In communicating this vision, it was also essential that we share our expected outcomes. Thanks to our extensive preparatory work, this was easy to do. A secondary goal was for the department to regularly engage, as a team, in professional development and enrichment activities, such as the preparatory book discussion for the Reboot. Meeting this goal would only serve to strengthen our abilities to provide the pedagogical leadership our administrators had charged us to do.

Of greatest concern for library administrators when it came to allowing an apparent halt of expected service was that all stakeholders affected were both informed and supportive of our plans. In my role as instruction coordinator, I met with our associate dean, answered their questions, and detailed our strategies for engaging our primary curricular partners in the PWR program with the Library Instruction Reboot. Thanks to a deliberate plan that our partners were able to endorse, we had administrative support of our project, provided we uphold our promise to continue clear communication about progress.

The Head of Library Learning Services lent constant support in this communication by publicly endorsing our work and helping to share our progress (Miller, 2019).

Curricular and Outreach Partners

Garnering the endorsement and participation of the PWR program stakeholders was the most critical piece to the Reboot's success. By 2018, Library Learning Services enjoyed a well-established relationship with the course leadership and instructors, which included integration of an annual library orientation for incoming course instructors and TAs, the annual Libraries Open House event and course-related instruction via one-shots for most sections of the course, which typically landed in the neighborhood of 90 sections. Our role in the course was well-respected, a foundation on which we sought to build our conversations about the Library Instruction Reboot and its impact on the ENGL 15 course and routine expectations of LLS.

Communication and engagement involved a layered approach, beginning with informational meetings and conversations among leadership from both units. This led to discussions about how to maintain curricular involvement and what forms it would take and culminated in the formation of a digital badges pilot within the course. The initial meeting between the LLS and PWR leadership teams was incredibly important, as it set the tone for the way the Reboot would be received and perceived as we moved forward. Our message was clear and concise, and conveyed our excitement. We wanted to

- re-envision our foundational information literacy program to use our expertise as effectively and meaningfully as possible,
- offer instruction in ways that most benefit our students, and
- do something a bit radical.

The excitement we conveyed was met by an equal level of enthusiasm from our teaching partners, which paved the way for us to engage them in the Reboot.

Before we could reach discussions about partnership in the project, however, we needed to make sure our colleagues teaching ENGL 15 felt adequately supported. We did not want anyone to feel we had completely jumped ship, leaving instructors with no way to support their students as they conducted their research papers. In collaboration with the curriculum developers for ENGL 15, we identified Credo Information Literacy Modules that could be integrated into the course syllabus at times when students would be preparing to conduct research (Penn State University Libraries, n.d.). The other primary mode of support we offered was research consultation via several possible contact points – our online live Ask a Librarian service offers options to request a consultation appointment, or to submit a question via email or chat. The LLS librarian responsible for liaison with ENGL 15 also developed some DIY lessons for the course instructors and would conduct a workshop at time-of-need to offer training. These plans were in place by the end of November, 2018, and the leadership of the PWR program agreed to email all course instructors with plenty of time for them to make preparations for their teaching in Spring 2019 accordingly [see appendix 2]. We, in turn, agreed to keep the PWR program in the loop on our progress, via a project blog [*Library Instruction Reboot*, 2019]. The fact that the PWR coordinators took a leadership role in communication signaled their endorsement of the Instruction Reboot, and further opened the doors for collaboration with individual instructors as we carried out our program recalibration.

Thanks to the PWR program's willing collaboration, we were able to carry out an evaluation of Credo Information Literacy Modules as vehicles for information literacy instruction; focus groups with ENGL 15 students; a revision of our library instruction evaluation practices and surveys; and a 12-course-section pilot using digital badges as a primary mode of delivering information literacy instruction.

Library Colleagues

In sharing the Library Instruction Reboot plans with our Libraries colleagues, who span the entire state of Pennsylvania and represent a cornucopia of specializations from technical services to scholarly communications, subject specialization, and everything in between, we took care to both anchor our project in institutional strategic plans and priorities, and to clearly articulate our plans to meet those objectives. In our project announcement, which we delivered in the middle of the fall 2018 semester (to allow time for questions and discussion), we also took care to explain why we had chosen to intentionally reduce our teaching load and communicate the project's endorsement by the PWR program leadership. Finally, we made a promise to "accountability and transparency," and invited our colleagues to follow along on our blog, where the announcement was also posted in its entirety (Behler, 2018). We kept this promise by announcing our regular blog updates via the Libraries weekly newsletter, and via several post-Reboot presentations during which we shared the lessons we learned, and what changes we'd made to our teaching program as a result of the experiment. Particularly important was articulating the ways in which these lessons could apply in other Penn State Library settings.

Well-Calculated Risk, Programmatic Rewards

Guided by the principles of doing what is meaningful, intentional, and relevant, the LLS teams proceeded to explore relationships with curricular and student engagement partners, rebalance our instruction commitments among multiple teaching modes, and identify opportunities and possible methods for future assessment of our instructional integrations so that we could continually assess our portfolio for meaningful integrations. Among key findings related to our foundational teaching was that, although we had articulated many possible foundational information literacy learning objectives, we were only teaching to two of them. We were also spending hours tailoring individual lessons for each requested library class, when, at the end of the day, the instructors were all looking for essentially the same outcomes. This led us to refine these two objectives, focused on evaluating sources and formulating research questions and creating keywords. We then created specific, shared lesson plans mapped to each. Doing so drastically cut the time required to prepare for classes! Instead of tweaking lessons on a case-by-case basis, we transitioned to an end-of-semester review and revise model.

The information literacy badges pilot for ENGL 15 yielded feedback that enabled us to devise an appropriate scale for offering badges as integrated course instruction. We also devised parameters for participation in the badging program, related to size of class and instructor experience teaching the course. Each semester, we now offer a first come, first served call for participation in an information literacy badges program that is supported by a Penn State Libraries-wide Badges Expert Team.

Through their exploration of Penn State's programs and courses for students from distinctive populations, the sub-team focused on supporting these students where and when they most need our help and identified several possible course integration opportunities. Since the Reboot, LLS has grown its support of the Penn

State Equity Scholars Program to include a personal librarian program and workshop opportunities. Information gathered also opened doors to supporting veteran students as well as additional multi-cultural student groups through outreach and engagement.

The Library Instruction Reboot experience also fundamentally changed the way the department structured its work. The three project teams morphed into long-term working teams, focused on Instruction and Pedagogy; Teaching, Innovation, and Online Learning; and Student Engagement and Outreach. Each team was able to build on their Reboot work, as well as incorporate lessons learned into the bigger picture of library instruction, student engagement, and outreach. This structure around our work also supported our formal recognition that teaching, via any mode, is of equal value and importance. These modes include, but are not limited to, face-to-face instruction, digital badges or microcredentials, online instruction, research consultation, and online learning object creation (Behler & Waltz, 2022). Finally, we developed a 'recipe' for successful partnerships (see Figure 9.1). These guidelines help us to evaluate existing and potential collaborations and enable us to make decisions about the level of support to give a particular initiative. As can often happen within a library instruction unit, we uncovered several "partnerships," in which LLS personnel were committing the lion's share of effort. Conducting this type of analysis can be difficult and time-consuming, but ultimately worthwhile when handled with care. Personnel capacity and concern for student needs must drive the decisions. One change that LLS made immediately, because of our Reboot findings, was to discontinue liaison work with the Effective Speech course. Over many years, we had sustained a significant amount of labor to support a course whose population and priorities had changed. We could continue to teach their dwindling number of library classes without continuing to engage in high-energy liaison practices with the department.

Recipe: Successful Partnerships
Ingredients:
Collaboration meets goals of library, department, and/or university strategic plan
Shared student-centered philosophy
Administrative support of all units involved
Collaborator is knowledgeable about how the library can help (or is willing to learn)
Impact of partnership can be assessed

FIGURE 9.1   A recipe for successful partnerships

A Lasting Impact

Thanks to the Library Instruction Reboot, flexibility and adaptation are the M.O. for Library Learning Services, more than ever before. We value and continue to seek out opportunities to *make space* – mentally, in our schedules, and in our routines – for design, analysis, evolution, and experimentation around our work. It is so easy to be too busy to think, create, innovate, or even rest. However, taking these actions is vital to a thriving information literacy program.

In 2020, we were all faced with an unthinkable challenge that turned the word "pivot" into a curse word. Penn State University classes were fully or mostly remote from March 2020 through August 2021. We had to quickly shift our instruction online, and we were very ready to do so. Thanks to the Reboot, we had standard lesson plans and prepared resources; the only difference was the mode. We had our teams, and the Teaching, Innovation, and Online Learning Team led the way in training our Penn State colleagues how to effectively teach on Zoom. The Instruction and Pedagogy Team worked to quickly create PowerPoint presentations to correspond with our standard lesson plans, and our student engagement and outreach program was able to continue virtually by pulling off a shift from an in-person library orientation for 3,000 students to a digital badge orientation that could be extended to any Penn State student in any location.

As the higher education environment continues to shift, mindfully and intentionally delivering library instruction is more important than ever. As information literacy coordinators, we can foster habit of mind among our colleagues by intentionally carving out space to be creative and thoughtful in our work and laying a flexible framework to guide us as we support our teaching colleagues and, above all, our students.

While putting a halt to teaching may not be achievable (or even necessary) in all cases, there are actions we can take to enable our colleagues to consider alternate ways of delivering library instruction. We can regularly schedule time to research and discuss alternate approaches to teaching; even a once per semester discussion can light a spark of inspiration. As coordinators, we can work directly with our curricular partners on our library colleagues' behalf; we can strive to develop clarity around curricular goals and move toward integrations that don't overly tax instructors or librarians, but that do effectively support our students. If, in our discussions, we discover that curricular needs have shifted or our partners no longer need us, we can adjust our efforts accordingly, making space for new and evolving needs to be met. Ultimately, we can build a stronger instruction program by taking a step back to identify where the true needs lie, and then following through with meaningful information literacy integrations.

References

Amsberry, D. (2019, February 1). Distinctive populations team introduction. *Library Instruction Reboot.* https://sites.psu.edu/libraryinstructionreboot/2019/02/01/distinctive-populations-team-introduction/

Association of College and Research Libraries. (2000). *Information literacy competency standards for higher education*. Association of College and Research Libraries.

Association of College and Research Libraries. (2015). *Framework for information literacy for higher education*. http://www.ala.org/acrl/standards/ilframework

Association of Research Libraries. (2018). *Research and analytics (assessment) program*. chrome-extension://efaidnbmnnnibpcajpcglclefindmkaj/https://www.arl.org/wp-content/uploads/2019/03/2018.09.25-ResearchLibraryImpactFramework.pdf

Behler, A. (2018, October 23). Time for a reboot! *Library Instruction Reboot*. https://sites.psu.edu/libraryinstructionreboot/2018/10/23/hello-world/

Behler, A., & Waltz, R.M. (2022). Stepping back from the line: How we stopped teaching and built a stronger program. *LOEX Conference Proceedings 2020*. 21. https://commons.emich.edu/loexconf2020/21/

Carbery, A., & Cottrell, J. (2014, May 10). *Inquiry-based learning online: Designing and delivering a blended and embedded information literacy program* [Presentation]. LOEX 2014: Creative visualization: The art of information literacy, Grand Rapids, MI. https://www.slideshare.net/acarbery/inquirybased-learning-online-designing-and-delivering-a-blended-and-embedded-information-literacy-program

Clossen, A. (2019, February 8). Foundational learners group introduction. *Library Instruction Reboot*. https://sites.psu.edu/libraryinstructionreboot/2019/02/08/foundational-learners-group-introduction/

Library Instruction Reboot: Re-visioning for library instruction. (2019). https://sites.psu.edu/libraryinstructionreboot/

Library Learning Services. (2018). *Instruction and outreach statistics* [Unpublished raw data].

McKeown, G. (2014). *Essentialism: The disciplined pursuit of less*. Virgin Books.

Miller, R.K. (2019, March 4). Instruction Reboot in three words: Intentional, meaningful, and strategic. *Library Instruction Reboot*. https://sites.psu.edu/libraryinstructionreboot/2019/03/04/instructional-reboot-in-three-words-intentional-meaningful-and-strategic/

Penn State Planning, Assessment, and Institutional Research. (n.d.). *Student enrollment*. Data Digest. Retrieved June 17, 2022, from https://datadigest.psu.edu/student-enrollment/

Penn State University Libraries. (2021). *Information literacy digital badges*. Online students use of the library. Retrieved June 17, 2022, from https://guides.libraries.psu.edu/c.php?g=516093&p=3540444

Penn State University Libraries. (n.d.). *Credo information literacy modules*. Retrieved June 21, 2022, from https://libraries.psu.edu/services/instruction-support/credo-information-literacy-modules

Raish, V. (2019, January 29). Digital badges sub team introduction and goals. *Library Instruction Reboot*. https://sites.psu.edu/libraryinstructionreboot/2019/01/29/digital-badges-sub-team-introduction-and-goals/

APPENDIX 1

Example Applications of Unique Library Instruction Integrations at Bristol Community College

The Causal Analysis

One of the professors who was early to adopt our new library instruction models assigned a causal analysis paper to his students each semester. This assignment required students to identify a trend, then find the cause and effect of that trend. While this seems straightforward, this assignment is consistently challenging for students to perform to the expectations of the professor.

What made this collaboration special was that the professor also encouraged his students to share their working Google Documents with the librarian so that the librarian could consult on their sources as they did research, in almost real time.

The first library class focused on identifying a workable trend that had clear evidence. Then, between the first and the second sessions, the students would share their Google Documents with us, posting the evidence they found. We would then check the sources the students provided and were often able to direct the students to more specific evidence using the comments feature. After this, the students would come back for a second session which focused on finding the causes and effects of the trend. We employed participatory learning and encouraged students to work together to think of potential causes and effects. Students were then directed to databases most applicable to their trend.

This faculty-librarian collaboration focused on the Framework concept of Inquiry. The partnership enabled both the instructor and the librarians to encourage students to think about asking questions based on what they were finding. In addition, the assignment allowed students to find causes and effects that they had not necessarily anticipated. This type of research enabled us to show students that research is meant to be an exploration and does not always have the expected outcome (Nadeau & Brown, 2016).

Lizzie Borden

Fall River may be famous for many things, but one of the most notorious was the vicious double murder of Andrew and Abby Borden in 1892. The accused, Lizzie Andrew Borden, was subsequently tried and acquitted in 1893, living out her days shunned by polite society in this small New England city. In fact, the Borden family gravesite lies not far from the campus in Fall River.

An instructor of Criminology decided to incorporate our enhanced model of information literacy in a way unique to our college, thanks to our proximity to this infamous double homicide. Using multi-sessions, we began to tour the murder scene with the students, who were divided into three teams: innocent, guilty, and verdict. The role of these teams was to investigate the murder through the lens of their team assignments, that is, guilty team would take the side of the prosecution, looking for evidence of Lizzie's guilt.

In the following weeks, the students met with librarians in the instruction classroom. The teams were be given contemporary evidence from the original investigation and trial. This included court transcripts, toxicology reports, and memoirs. They were also provided access to a research guide (Brown, 2020) and archival material pulled specifically for each team to consider.

The college archives are full of resources on the Borden murders, including items written by both the defense and the prosecution. These were provided to each team respectively. We own several books proclaiming either Lizzie's innocence or guilt. The verdict team had access to the arguments on both sides to make their decision.

In the end, the guilty and innocent team presented their cases to the jury team, who decided Lizzie's posthumous fate. Often, they acquit her just as she was acquitted in 1893.

The Psych Experiment

An instructor within the Psychology Department worked with our Attleboro librarian to create an in-depth class on reading an experimental research paper (Devane et al., 2018). Often students enter college with no understanding of the design or intent of a scholarly peer-reviewed article. As such, the instructor required her freshman-level class to imagine and write up a psychological experiment proposal as if they were going to complete and publish the study.

We used two class sessions to dissect the article and then instructed on how to find supporting evidence. In the first session, students were taught the different components of a psychological article (identifying the hypothesis, operational definitions, experimental design, participants, the control, independent and dependent variables, etc.) and how to locate them in the print article. We used the second session to locate articles supporting their hypothesis.

The Big Question and Infographics

The English Department at Bristol Community College is full of faculty who are interested in innovative pedagogy. A long-time professor at the college has explored reading and writing using different genres in the class assignments. The major assignments of the course focused on different audiences, genres, and rhetorical situations (Tinberg, 2017).

The librarians attended two sessions of the class. The first session focused on finding scholarly evidence to help answer a "big question." Later in the semester, the librarians returned to the classroom to help students learn how to communicate the answer to their big question (initially answered in a ten-page paper) in an infographic. Librarians introduced different infographic development programs like *Canva* (https://www.canva.com) and *Piktochart* (https://piktochart.com). The librarians walked students through how to create an infographic and communicate effectively in this very specific genre.

The long-term benefit of this collaboration has impacted more than students. Through this partnership, librarians have learned new and innovative ways to communicate their impact outside of a traditional institutional report or paper.

References

Brown, E. (2020). *CRJ251: Criminology (Mayhew)*. https://libguides.bristolcc.edu/crj251/mayhew

Devane, N., Richter, L., & Brown, E. (2018, March 7). *Collaborative design: Faculty and librarian partnerships for integrated information literacy* [Conference presentation]. Bristol Academic Lecture Series.

Nadeau, J.P., & Brown, E. (2016, October 10). *Encouraging research as inquiry: An instructor-librarian collaboration* [Conference presentation]. Bristol Academic Lecture Series.

Tinberg, H. (2017). Teaching for transfer: A passport for writing in new contexts. *New Frontiers in Writing*, *19*(1). https://www.aacu.org/peerreview/2017/Winter/Tinberg

APPENDIX 2

Email Announcing Reboot to ENGL 15 Instructors

TO: Program in Writing and Rhetoric Instructors

FROM: Office of the Program in Writing and Rhetoric

DATE: November 29, 2018

SUBJECT: Spring 2019 LLS Hiatus

Dear Colleagues,

The PWR Office would like to inform all PWR course instructors of an important change to the typical availability of Library Learning Services (LLS) for the coming Spring 2019 semester. To better meet the needs of the instructors and students whom they serve, LLS will take a hiatus from face-to-face teaching and dedicate the spring 2019 semester to a Library Instruction Reboot. This reboot will directly affect the English Department in that the traditional library instruction sessions for PWR courses will not be offered during the Spring 2019 semester. Instead, the PWR Office, along with LLS, encourages you to take advantage of the following options for assisting your students with library and information literacy instruction:

- Credo Information Literacy Modules: These are online, interactive modules that include videos, tutorials, and quizzes on research skills ranging from under-standing the research process to searching effectively to evaluating and citing sources. If you would like to incorporate a few of these modules into your class sections, they can be found through the libraries' website at https://libraries.psu.edu/services/instruction-support/credo-information-literacy-modules.
- Individualized Research Consultation: This service allows students to contact the library and schedule research consultation appointments on an as-needed basis.

LLS welcomes your support and questions. You can read more about their project and follow along with their progress at https://sites.psu.edu/libraryinstructionreboot/. If you have questions about either of the above services, you are welcome to get in touch with anyone from the LLS team.

Should you need further assistance, the PWR Office will be happy to make suggestions about how you can best incorporate the Credo Information Literacy Modules into your Spring 2019 course in place of the typical library instruction workshops; please don't hesitate to reach out to us.

Happy Holidays!
The PWR Office

INDEX

Note: **Bold** page numbers refer to tables and *italic* page numbers refer to figures.

AAC&U *Information Literacy VALUE Rubric* 11, 36–37, 138–139
AASL. *See* American Association of School Librarians (AASL)
Academic Writing Program (AWP), UMD Libraries 64, 65–66, 72; Teaching Assistants and 67–68
ACRL. *See* Association for College & Research Libraries (ACRL)
administrative models 1
ALA. *See* American Library Association (ALA)
American Association of School Librarians (AASL) 28
American Library Association (ALA) 10
American Library Association Presidential Committee on Information Literacy: Final Report on IL (1989) 28
ARCS Model 57
Articulate Rise software 104, 107
assessment: culture of, at URI 35–38; data, Student Learning Assessment Plan 118–122, 124; mandate 12–13; student learning (*See* Student Learning Assessment Plan)
Association for College & Research Libraries (ACRL) 2; *Characteristics of Programs of Information Literacy that Illustrate Best Practices: A Guideline* 38, 45, 49, 50; *Framework for Information Literacy in Higher Education* 2, 9, 17–19, **18**, 33,

37, 46, 90, 140, **143**; Immersion Program 2–3, 32; *Information Literacy Competency Standards for Higher Education* 2, 10–12, 13, 28, 34, 37, 45–46; Research Planning and Review Committee 55; *Roles and Strengths of Teaching Librarians* 53, 55; *Standards for Proficiencies for Instruction Librarians and Coordinators: A Practical Guide* (2008) 3, 37
asynchronous online tutorials 40, 86
AWP. *See* Academic Writing Program (AWP)

Badke, W. 85
Bay Area Community College (BACC) Information Competency Proficiency Exam 36
Bayhawks Vote workshops 144
Beaudet, Mike 146
Benya-Soderbom, Rebecca 146
bibliographic analysis 13
bibliographic instruction 10. *See also* information literacy
BIOL 05LA 100, 101, 102, *102*, *103*, *108*; "Thinking Like a Scientist" module 107–109, 111
Blackboard 88, 92, 93
Blinstrub, Ashley 4
Borden, Abby 163
Borden, Andrew 163

Borden, Lizzie Andrew 163
Brasley, S.S. 85
Breivik, Patricia Senn 10
Bristol Community College, information literacy: Assessment Rubric **141–143**; chaser sessions 139; collaboration for innovation 140, 144; college-wide colloquia 145–146; example applications of unique library instruction integrations 162–164; learning communities 147; misinformation/meme workshops 145; overview 137; The Poisoned Path Project 147; transforming the Framework into a rubric 140; VALUE rubric 138–139; voting rights 144
Brown, Emily 4, 137, 147
Bruce, Christine 16, 21n1

Canva 164
"capstone" skills 140
Carbery, Alan 152
categories of work 49–50
causal analysis 162
Characteristics of Programs of Information Literacy that Illustrate Best Practices: A Guideline 38, 45, 49, 50
chaser sessions 139
CHEM 01LA 100–101, 102, 102, 103, 103–107, 106–107
Chronicle of Higher Education 47, 48
CNAS. See College of Agricultural and Natural Sciences (CNAS)
collaboration and partnerships: beyond the library 60; C&I Center, CSP library 91–93; faculty-librarian collaborations 85, 162; instruction coordinator in curriculum partnerships 93–95; in the library 58–60; recipe for successful partnerships 159
College of Agricultural and Natural Sciences (CNAS) 100, 101, 112n1
community college, IL education in 137–138; challenges 138. See also Bristol Community College, information literacy
community of practice (COP) approach: Fearless Teaching Institute 65, 69, 76–79; in higher education 70; intentional cultivation of community 80; in libraries 70–71; literature review 69–70; overview 15–16; Research and Teaching Fellowship 64, 69, 71–75; Student Learning Assessment Community of Practice 131; UMD

Libraries 69–75. See also informed learning approach
Concordia University, St. Paul (CSP) library: background 87; C&I Center 87–89; expanded work and partnerships 91–93; instruction program 89–91
Cook, Dani Brecher 4
COP. See community of practice (COP) approach
Cottrell, Janet 152
course development 28–33
COVID-19 pandemic: Library Instruction Reboot and 160; misinformation and 145, 146; online instruction and 111
Cox, J. 86
CRC Handbook of Chemistry and Physics 101, 103, 104, 105, 106
CREATE-style assignment 108, 109
Credo Information Literacy Modules 157, 165
Critical Data Studies Collective 20
critical information literacy 19–20
Curriculum and Instruction Center (C&I Center), CSP library: expanded work and partnerships 91–93; overview 87; work 88–89
curriculum development and design: C&I Center (See Curriculum and Instruction Center (C&I Center), CSP library); collaborations, questions to consider 95–96; information literacy instruction (ILI) and 85, 86; instruction coordinator in curriculum partnerships 93–95; multi-modal curriculum 102
curriculum map, Student Learning Assessment 129–130, **130**

data policies: revised Student Learning Assessment Plan 128; Student Learning Assessment Plan 121
Delaleu, Rob 146
digital literacy 14–15. See also information literacy
Digital Literacy Framework Toolkit 15
DiMarzio, Denise 145
Distinctive Populations 155
Dolinger, Elizabeth 39
Douglas, Veronica Arellano 48, 68
Drabinski, Emily 12, 19
Dyson, Allan J.: on library instruction 1–2

EDUCAUSE Horizon Reports 55
Elmborg, James 19
Ettarh, Fobazi 51

faculty-librarian collaborations 85, 162.
See also curriculum development and
design
fake news 145
Farrell, R. 85
Fearless Teaching Institute (FTI) 65, 69,
76–79; mutual engagement and
community 77–78; shared enterprise 77;
shared repertoire 78–79. *See also* Research
and Teaching Fellowship (RTF)
Feliú-Mójer, Mónica, Dr. 146
Fontainha, E. 71
Foundational Learners 154–155
foundational learning objectives, for library
instruction 154
*Framework for Information Literacy in Higher
Education* 2, 9, 17–19, **18**, 33, 37, 90;
practical implications of 46; transforming
the Framework into a rubric 140
Frechette, Steve 146
Freire, P. 19
fundraising 17, 59

Gadsby, Joanna 48, 68
Gannon-Leary, P. 71
General Education Program, URI 31–32,
36–37
General Education Revision Task Force
(GERTF) 36
GERTF. *See* General Education Revision
Task Force (GERTF)
GeST windows model 16
Graduate School of Library and Information
Studies (GSLIS), URI 29
GSLIS. *See* Graduate School of Library and
Information Studies (GSLIS), URI
Guimont, Eddie 146

Habib, Farah 145
Haldeman, Lisa 40
2022 *Harvard Business Review* 47, 48, 50, 52
Head, Allison, Dr. 145
higher education, IL in: COPs in 70;
education curriculum, developing a place
for 26–41; note on changes in 35;
overview 9–21. *See also* information
literacy (IL)
Hogan, Laura 145–146
Hughes, S.K. 27

ILI. *See* information literacy
instruction (ILI)
ILSES. *See* Information Literacy Self-
Efficacy Scale (ILSES)

ILT. *See* Information Literacy Test (ILT)
individual roles, scoping 53–57
Infobase's Credo Information Literacy-
Core modules (InfoLit-Core) 90, 91
infographic development programs 164
InfoLit-Core. *See* Infobase's Credo
Information Literacy-Core modules
(InfoLit-Core)
information literacy (IL): *vs.* bibliographic
instruction 10; critical 19–20; in higher
education 9–21; in the higher education
curriculum, developing a place for
26–41; instructional modes into 98–112;
international conference, in Prague 10;
origin of, Zurkowski and 9–10; other
approaches to 15–17; standardization
years 10–12; teaching practice,
constraining 12; at URI (*See* University
of Rhode Island (URI)); VALUE
Rubrics for 11, 138–139
Information Literacy as a Liberal Art 27
*Information Literacy Competency Standards for
Higher Education* 10–11, 34, 45–46
information literacy instruction (ILI) 85;
challenges faced 85–86; CSP library
instruction program 89.
See also curriculum development and
design
Information Literacy Microcourse 40
information literacy (IL) plan: course
development to 33–35; guiding
documents for 27–28; mission statement
and 27; vision statement and 27–28
Information Literacy Self-Efficacy Scale
(ILSES) 13
Information Literacy Test (ILT) 13
information literate person 10
Information Studies 39
informed learning approach 16–17.
See also community of practice approach
informed learning design 17
Institute of Museum and Library
Services 17
instruction coordinators: campus discussions
and 15; hiring 1; role in curriculum
partnerships 93–95
instructional support: BIOL 05LA 100, 101,
103, 107–109, *108*; CHEM 01LA 100,
102, *102*, *103*, 103–107, *106–107*;
demand for 98–99; establishing the need
99–100; NASC 093 100, 102, *102*, *103*,
109–110, *110*; pandemic and 111
IT Learning Management System (LMS)
staff 87, 88, 92

Jackman, Lana 10
Jacobson, T.E. 15
JISC model 15
Johnson, A. 86
Jones, Brett 57

Kapitzke, Cushla 19
Keene State College (KSC) 39–40
Keller, John 57
Kim, J. 71
Kirk, Tom 33
Kirker, Maoria J. 4
Koltay, T. 14

Launch Certificate, TLTC 76, 78
Lave, Jean 69
learning communities, Bristol Community
    College and 147
learning management system (LMS) 88, 91,
    92, 99
learning outcomes 36–38, 86, 91, 92, 94,
    98, 102, 109, 121–122, 127–128,
    140, 154
Lencioni, Patrick 48
liaison librarians 59, 85–86
LIB 120: Introduction to Information
    Literacy 30, 31, 32, 35, 36
LIB 140: Special Topics in Information
    Literacy 30, 31
LibGuides 90, 91, 92, 93
librarianship: core values of 51; *Standards*
    and 12; transliteracy in, application of 14
library administration, support from 80, 156
library curriculum map 129–130, **130**
library instruction programs: boundaries,
    decisions on 49; Dyson and 1;
    foundation (*See* library instruction
    programs, foundation); instruments and
    tools 52; mission and vision statement
    and 50–51; roles (*See* roles, library
    instruction team); scope of work 49;
    team (*See* team and work, scoping).
    See also information literacy (IL)
library instruction programs, foundation:
    individual roles, scoping 53–57;
    overview 46; planning, prioritizing, and
    partnering 57–60; scoping the team and
    the work 46–53
Library Instruction Reboot 153, 155, 165;
    communication about 155–158
Library Learning Services (LLS) 45, 50,
    151–152, 156, 157, 165; goals 153
Life Values Inventory tool 52

Lipmanowicz, Henri 51
LLS. *See* Library Learning Services (LLS)
LMS. *See* learning management
    system (LMS)
LMS staff 87, 88, 92
LOEX Library Instruction Conference,
    2001 2
LOEX organization: annual conference,
    2014 152long-term goals 57–58

MacDonald, Mary C. 3
Mackey, T.P. 15
Manning, Katharine 47
Mason Library, KSC 39
Masters of Library and Information Science
    (MLIS) students 69, 71, 73, 74
Maybee, Clarence 3
McCandless, Keith 51
McElroy, Kelly 19
McKeown, Greg 153
McKillop Library, Salve Regina
    University 40
McVeigh, Timothy 28–29
Media and Information Literacy (MIL) 14
media literacy 9, 14. *See also* information
    literacy
meme workshops 145
metaliteracy model 17
MGT 110: Introduction to Business
    course 31
Middleton, Cheryl 64
MIL. *See* Media and Information
    Literacy (MIL)
M.I.L.E. *See* Mills Information Literacy
    Evaluation (M.I.L.E.)
Mills Information Literacy Evaluation
    (M.I.L.E.) 12
misinformation workshops 145
mission statement: IL plan and 27; library
    instruction programs and 50–51
MLIS. *See* Masters of Library and
    Information Science (MLIS) students
Moran, C. 86
multi-modal curriculum 102
multiple choice tests 13
multi-sessions 139
multi-tiered system 139
Mulvihill, R. 86
MUSIC model 57
mutual engagement and community:
    Fearless Teaching Institute (FTI) 77–78;
    Research and Teaching Fellowship
    (RTF) 74

NASC 093 100, 102, *102*, *103*, 109–110, *110*

National Commission on Libraries and Information Science (NCLIS) 10

National Forum on Information Literacy (NFIL) 10

NCLIS. *See* National Commission on Libraries and Information Science (NCLIS)

NEASC. *See* New England Association of Schools & Colleges (NEASC)

NECHE. *See* New England Commission of Higher Education (NECHE)

Neely, Teresa 12

New England Association of Schools & Colleges (NEASC) 34, 35

New England Commission of Higher Education (NECHE) 34, 35, 98

NFIL. *See* National Forum on Information Literacy (NFIL)

Norlin, Elaina 48

Northeast Campus (TCC) 40–41

OER. *See* open educational resources (OER)

Office of Student Learning and Outcomes Assessment and Accreditation (SLOAA) Committee, URI 36, 37

on-campus partnership 147

"one-shot" instruction model 4, 32, 35, 38, 39, 86, 139; efficacy 98–99

online tutorials: asynchronous 40, 86; Blackboard LMS 100

open educational resources (OER) 89

Pagowsky, Nicole 19

pandemic. *See* COVID-19 pandemic

partnerships and collaboration: beyond the library 60; C&I Center, CSP library 91–93; faculty-librarian collaborations 85, 162; instruction coordinator in curriculum partnerships 93–95; in the library 58–60; recipe for successful partnerships *159*

Pawley, Christine 19

peer observations, in RTF 74

Penn State Equity Scholars Program 158–159

Penn State Library: administration 156; background 151–152; curricular and outreach partners 156–157; Library Instruction Reboot and 158–159, 160

person-centered leadership 48

Petrowski, M.J. 2–3

Piktochart 164

PIL. *See* Project Information Literacy (PIL) studies

"Pizza and Politics" program 144

planning 57–60; priorities and strategic planning 58

The Poisoned Path Project 147

post-observation consultations 74

Prague Declaration 10

pre-observation surveys 74

Presidential Committee on Information Literacy 10

priorities, establishing 58

program boundaries, categories of work 49

program development 4

Program in Writing and Rhetoric (PWR), Penn State University 154, 156, 165

Project Information Literacy (PIL) studies 13

Project SAILS 13

psychological safety 48

Putin, Vladimir 146

PWR. *See* Program in Writing and Rhetoric (PWR)

Qualtrics-based quiz 101, 103, 105, 109

RACI charts *54*, 54–55

RAD. *See* Researching Across the Disciplines (RAD)

Rapien, Mary 146

Research and Teaching Fellowship (RTF) 64, 69, 71–75; mutual engagement and community 74; shared enterprise 73–74; shared repertoire 75; student teachers and 73; "Teaching as Research" project 76. *See also* Fearless Teaching Institute (FTI)

Research Path tutorial 40

Researching Across the Disciplines (RAD) seminar 39

Richter, Lisa 40

roles, library instruction team: continued learning and succession planning 56–57; defining and communicating roles 53–55; individual roles 53–57; RACI charts *54*, 54–55; role evolution 55–56

Roles and Strengths of Teaching Librarians, ACRL 53, 55

RTF. *See* Research and Teaching Fellowship (RTF)

RTF Alumni Network 74

Sachs, Dianna 40

safety and trust 47–48

Salve Regina University 40

"sample job description" 1

75 Tools for Creative Thinking 51
Shapiro, J.J. 27
shared enterprise: Fearless Teaching
    Institute (FTI) 77; Research and
    Teaching Fellowship (RTF) 73–74
shared repertoire: Fearless Teaching
    Institute (FTI) 78–79; Research and
    Teaching Fellowship (RTF) 75
shared vision, developing 46
short-term goals 57
Sitar, Meghan 19
Six Frames 16
*The Six-Step Guide to Library Worker
    Engagement* 48
SLOAA. *See* Office of Student Learning and
    Outcomes Assessment and Accreditation
    (SLOAA) Committee, URI
SLOs. *See* student learning outcomes
    (SLOs)
Souza-Mort, Susan 4, 137, 145
standardization years 10–12
*Standards for Proficiencies for Instruction
    Librarians and Coordinators: A Practical
    Guide* (2008), ACRL's 3
STEM courses pathway 102, *102*
strategic planning 58
strengths, weaknesses, opportunities, and
    threats (SWOT) analysis 72
StrengthsFinder 2.0 tool 52
Student Learning Assessment Community
    of Practice 131
Student Learning Assessment Plan:
    assessment data 124; developing the
    original 118–122; evaluation of
    assessment reports 131; feedback and
    training 123; Library Curriculum Map
    129–130, **130**; library instructors,
    reception by 124–125; overview 118;
    review of 125–126; revised 126–128;
    structure of 119–122
Student Learning Assessment Toolkit 129
succession planning 56–57
Succession Planning Toolkit (University of
    Washington) 57
SWOT. *See* strengths, weaknesses,
    opportunities, and threats (SWOT)
    analysis

TAs. *See* Teaching Assistants (TAs)
Task Force for Teaching and Research, IL
    plan 33
TATIL. *See* Threshold Achievement Test
    for Information Literacy (TATIL)

Teaching and Learning Services (TLS) 65,
    68, 71–72
Teaching and Learning Transformation
    Center (TLTC), UMD 76; Launch
    Certificate 76, 78
Teaching Assistants (TAs): Academic
    Writing Program and 67–68; defined 67;
    RTF program and 73
"teach-ins" 146
team power structures 47
Tewell, Eamon 19
Texas Information Literacy Tutorial (TILT)
    11–12
"Thinking Like a Scientist" module, BIOL
    05LA 107–109, 111
Thomas, Sue 14
"3 T's: Exploring New Frontiers in
    Teaching, Technology and Transliteracy
    Conference" 14
three-credit IL course 29–30
Threshold Achievement Test for
    Information Literacy (TATIL) 13
threshold concepts theory 17–18, **18**
TILT. *See* Texas Information Literacy
    Tutorial (TILT)
TLS. *See* Teaching and Learning
    Services (TLS)
TLTC. *See* Teaching and Learning
    Transformation Center (TLTC)
transliteracy 14
trauma, defined 47
trauma-informed leadership 47, 48
trauma-informed workplaces 47
trust and safety 47–48
Tulsa Community College (TCC) 40–41
tutorials: M.I.L.E. 12; online 11, 40, 86,
    100, *106*, 108; video 91
2019 *Strategic Planning for Academic Libraries:
    A Step-by-Step Guide* 58

"underground" library instruction 1
UNESCO. *See* United Nations
    Educational, Scientific and Cultural
    Organization (UNESCO)
United Nations Educational, Scientific and
    Cultural Organization (UNESCO)
    10, 14
University of California, Riverside (UC
    Riverside) Library, instructional support:
    demand for 98–99; establishing the need
    99–100; evaluation and iteration
    110–111; multi-modal curriculum 102;
    reestablish relationships 100–102

University of Maryland (UMD) Libraries:
Academic Writing Program and 64,
65–66; community of practice 64,
69–75; Fearless Teaching Institute 65,
76–79; overview 65; Research and
Teaching Fellowship (RTF) 64, 71–75;
Teaching and Learning Services (TLS)
65, 68; Teaching and Learning
Transformation Center (TLTC) 76; User
Education Services (UES) 66
University of Rhode Island (URI): course
development 28–33; culture of assessment
at 35–38; General Education Program
31–32, 36; Graduate School of Library and
Information Studies (GSLIS) 29; IL Rubric
37; Learning Outcomes Oversight
Committee (LOOC) 37; mission statement
27; Office of Student Learning and
Outcomes Assessment and Accreditation
(SLOAA) Committee 36, 37
University of Rhode Island Mission
Statement 27
User Education Services (UES), UMD
Libraries 66

Valid Assessment of Learning in
Undergraduate Education (VALUE)
Rubrics 11, 37, 138–139
values 51–52
video tutorials 91
vision statement: IL plan and 27–28; library
instruction programs and 50–51

Waldo Library, WMU 40
Waltz, Rebecca Miller 3
WASC Senior College and University
Commission 98
Weiner, Sharon 10
Weisberger, Ron, Dr. 146, 147
Wenger, Etienne 69, 70
Western Association of Schools and
Colleges (WASC) 98
Western Michigan University (WMU) 40
Wightman, Rachel I. 4
Worthington, Robyn 146
"wounded workgroups" 47

Zoom session 92, 111
Zurkowski, Paul 9

For Product Safety Concerns and Information please contact our EU
representative GPSR@taylorandfrancis.com Taylor & Francis Verlag GmbH,
Kaufingerstraße 24, 80331 München, Germany

Printed and bound by CPI Group (UK) Ltd, Croydon, CR0 4YY
08/06/2025
01896986-0020